INTRODUCTION

A number of these chapters were delivered as lectures. "Wrestling with an Angel" was the first Bishop Agnellus Andrew Lecture delivered in the Concert Hall of Broadcasting House in October 1990; "Minstrel for the Television Age" was an address given at a Commemoration of Charles Wesley at the New Room, Bristol in 1988; "The Theology of the Nine O'Clock News" is an amended version of my 1986 Hibbert Lecture; "The Debate about Religious Broadcasting" formed the basis of the 1990 St Cuthbert's Day Lecture at St Cuthbert's Church, Edinburgh. I am grateful for permission to reproduce them. Because so many of these chapters were originally spoken I have retained the style of conversational speech.

I have two acknowledgements to make; one general, the other particular. Over the years, my colleagues in the BBC have taught me all I know about broadcasting. I have been greatly enriched by their friendship and experience. And Dr Pauline Webb has put me once more in her debt by subjecting the manuscript to her usual sympathetic but rigorous examination. As an editor, she combines charm and ruthlessness in equal proportions; the reader has been spared a number of obscurities and infelicities as a result.

Colin Morris

WRESTLING WITH AN ANGEL

There can be few preachers of the Gospel who have had so varied a career as Colin Morris. Entering the Methodist ministry after national service as a marine commando, his first appointment was to the South Yorkshire Coalfields mission, where his concern for industrial relations led him to a period of research at Nuffield College, Oxford. From there he was appointed to work as a missionary in the copperbelt of Central Africa. Caught up in the maelstrom of African struggles for independence, he took on a role of political leadership and, as a close supporter of Kenneth Kaunda, participated in the constitutional talks that led to the foundation of the new nation of Zambia, where he was elected as the first President of the United Church of Zambia.

His international reputation as a preacher led to his being invited to return to Britain to occupy the pulpit of Wesley's Chapel in London, and subsequently to his election as President of the British Methodist Conference. In the tradition of Wesley himself "the world became his parish" when he was appointed General Secretary of the Overseas Division of the Methodist Church.

Meanwhile, first in Zambia and later in Britain, he had been quick to recognize the value of the mass media of communication and became a frequent and popular broadcaster and television presenter. In 1978 he was appointed Head of Religious Broadcasting at the BBC, from where he moved on to his present office as Controller of the BBC, Northern Ireland. In this demanding post, he has continued to monitor developments within the media and has also contributed personally with great distinction to services of worship on television and to radio talks and discussions.

Thus in this, the latest of a score of books, he writes as both a practitioner and a theologian, whose reflections on the significance of the modern media of communication are reinforced by his own wit, wisdom and remarkable gifts as a preacher of the Christian Gospel.

COLIN MORRIS

WRESTLING WITH AN ANGEL

REFLECTIONS ON CHRISTIAN COMMUNICATION

COLLINS

FOUNT PAPERBACKS

William Collins Sons & Co. Ltd
London . Glasgow . Sydney . Auckland
Toronto . Johannesburg

First published in Great Britain in 1990 by Fount Paperbacks
Fount Paperbacks is an imprint of
Collins Religious Division,
part of the Collins Publishing Group
8 Grafton Street, London W1X 3LA

Phototypeset by Input Typesetting Ltd, London
Printed and bound in Great Britain by William Collins
Sons & Co. Ltd., Glasgow

This book is for
Jean Palk
With love and gratitude

CONTENTS

ONE

WRESTLING WITH AN ANGEL

The story is one of the original forms of communication. So here is an old Bible story which bursts with insights about the nature of religious communication. According to Genesis 32, Jacob wrestles all night with an unknown adversary by the ford at the River Jabbok. One tradition identifies the stranger as an angel, an embodiment of divine communication. By the time the sun rises and Jacob's opponent leaves him, several things have happened. He has a new name appropriate to his future, he has a good idea who his adversary is, and he has been crippled in the struggle.

What does all this say about religious communication? Certainly, that mutual disclosure is the key to it. It is an encounter, even a collision, between personalities who, whatever they learn by way of information, discover more about each other and about themselves as a result.

And if the meeting should be a Divine/human encounter, then God's self-disclosure is always veiled, mysterious – it is never without ambiguity. When his opponent leaves him, Jacob is still not *quite* sure with whom he has been dealing – "Why do you ask my name?", enquires the stranger. Yet Jacob guessed that he had encountered God and lived to tell the tale.

And communication is a painful and costly business.

Jacob emerges from the encounter with a pronounced limp, even though he had wrestled God to a draw and received his blessing. God seemed to be saying, "By all means meet me in mutual disclosure, provided you are prepared to pay the price."

Let's look at this story in detail.

Our Gregarious God

God seeks out Jacob. He encounters him on the patriarch's own ground. This is a God who relishes company, who is gregarious, who finds the solitary eminence of the Heaven of Heavens a lonely place. He is a God we might stumble upon as though by accident at a ford by the River Jabbok; who shirks no encounter, however close.

Consider the possibility of a God who is tight-lipped by nature; who sits in heaven keeping his own counsel like Rodin's *Thinker*, preoccupied with whatever private thoughts flit through the mind of a lonely Deity. Then consider creatures who have no capacity or appetite for reaching out towards the one in whom they live, move and have their being; who are hopelessly earthed in their thoughts and imagination. Either possibility, a laconic God or sense-bound creatures, would render most of the higher religions unnecessary.

The higher religions, note. Even an uncommunicative God may be perceived as naked power, and placated by magical rites and religious observances to ward off the worst consequences of his arbitrary behaviour. But the notion of a talkative God takes religion onto a different plane, occupied most notably by Christianity, its elder brother Judaism and its younger cousin Islam. They share the belief that God is given to gracious acts of self-disclosure.

The most substantial evidence of God's talkativeness is the universe itself. Communication was the original creative impulse – "In the beginning was the Word". God spoke creation into existence – "And God said, 'Let there be light!' and there was light." Lawyers talk of "uttering" a document. They are following an irreproachable precedent – God uttered the universe.

The universe, then, is an expression of God's mind. According to Christianity, its central history embodies an account of the establishment, breakdown and restoration of Divine/human communication. God creates Adam and immediately starts up a conversation with him. And he gives Adam a companion, Eve, because "it is not good for him to be alone". Adam needs someone with whom he can reproduce the pattern of communication God has established as the house style of the created order.

For human beings to be "made in God's image" must mean to share his urge towards self-disclosure since there are not many other ways in which they could be replicas of an invisible Deity. The created order is divided into those elements that are able to emulate God's self-disclosure and those that cannot. It is the language line which separates human beings from the beasts. Indeed, the condition of people who shrink from self-disclosure, who have locked themselves away from human encounter, is usually regarded as pathological. They suffer a diminished humanity.

God's self-disclosure is more than the passing on of interesting ideas in his mind or news about his intentions. Herein lies the distinction between two terms we tend to use interchangeably – information and communication.

Information is the passing on of bits of intelligence from the one who knows to the one who would know – the communication *of*. It is not necessarily a human function at all; two computer terminals would do the trick. **Communication**, however, is the self-disclosure of the two parties in the act of passing on these bits of intelligence – communication *between*. The essence of true communication, therefore, is sharing. Hence, George Gerbner, Professor of Communications in the University of Pennsylvania, defines communication as "social intercourse regulated by means of messages".

This view of communication reaches its highest expression in Christianity's claim that what is passed on from God to human beings is not knowledge, however profound, but life, and not just life but divine life through Jesus Christ. Christian communication is not concerned with bits of intelligence passing between God and human beings, like a letter delivered by post or tidings sent buzzing down a telephone wire. The message is nothing less than a partial unveiling of God's nature. Christ is the communicated self-expression of God.

When the Canadian philosopher of communication, Marshall McLuhan, insisted that the medium is the message, this insight struck home with the force of a revelation. Yet nineteen centuries before him the Bible had made just that claim about Jesus: that he is both medium and message. When the New Testament writers talked of "preaching Christ" or "preaching the Gospel" or "preaching salvation", they were not referring to three separate things but highlighting the identity between medium and message from three different perspectives.

The Whisper of God's Ways

The practical purpose of theology is to make it possible for the Gospel to be heard in our time. It must therefore offer solutions to specific problems that might hinder God's self-disclosure. Whatever else it is, Christian doctrine must be a system of communication.

Take the Trinity. It tackles head-on the question: how can a God whose nature is self-disclosure be solitary? Christian orthodoxy says that the social nature of God is part of his eternal essence; it is not expressed through attributes which develop over time. There has never been a time when God was alone. Indeed – daring to quote God's own words about Adam against him – if it is not good that a man should be alone, still less is it desirable that God should be solitary. For how could he express himself except as a voice that echoes round the vaults of Heaven and returns as hollow acquiescence? There is no one there to respond. Those metaphysical attributes of God beloved of the classical theologians – omnipotence, omniscience and omnipresence – are mere abstractions unless expressed in terms of relationship. For they are qualities that need acknowledgement.

If the essential Christian message is that of God's self-disclosure, then the Trinity shows how it is done. Father, Son and Holy Spirit obviously do not communicate by passing on information to one another like friends chatting on a three-way phone. They express their essential selves through love; their fiery gaze is enough. Taken with absolute seriousness, the Trinitarian model implies that the essential precondition for all true communication is love. The urge to give, to share, to cherish – in short, to communicate – is the rationale of the created order because it is the expression of the inner dynamic of the Triune God.

Information, orders, instructions, commands can be issued in a spirit of hostility, superiority or indifference. But the only context in which the parties are prepared to open themselves to each other, to engage in honest self-disclosure, is one where there is that degree of mutuality we call love.

When Jacob at Peniel asked for a blessing, he sought God's assurance that through struggle, contention and pain, they had won through to a relationship of loving trust. And when God blessed Jacob he was confirming that there had been a genuine personal encounter, heart had reached out to heart.

Communication, then, is not just concerned with facts, but with what Paul called *the truth in love*. Only in this way can communication in a fallen world remain uncorrupted by considerations of power and self-seeking. For love communicates itself; the more intense it is, the less it requires special techniques to project it. Its meaning is transparent; its impact is unmistakable.

Another essential condition for true communication is equality. This is not to say there can only be real communication in a totally egalitarian society. Equality in the act of communication means that the parties acknowledge their unconditional willingness to give and receive – their reciprocal need of what the other has to offer. How can this be possible when the exchange is between an omnipotent God and a mortal creature? The answer of Christian doctrine is the Incarnation. As Calvin put it, "God bends down, and lowering himself, lisps into our ear that we might hear and understand."

God confronts Jacob at Peniel not as a pillar of fire nor a blinding light, but as a man. In a dress rehearsal for the Incarnation, he seems to divest himself of his divinity; in

Charles Wesley's image, God is "contracted to a span, incomprehensibly made man".

The act of communication becomes a struggle between equals, the balance of advantage swinging now this way, now that. God limits his strength, or as is the way in legends about heroes wrestling with gods, Jacob draws power from his supernatural adversary. Yet it is at the point of Jacob's greatest weakness, as his strength is ebbing, that he learns the truth denied him when he is still strong. Thus, according to the prophet Hosea's commentary on the story, "Jacob fought against an angel and won. He wept and asked for a blessing" (12:4).

The experience of Jacob at Peniel is an uncanny foreshadowing of Jesus' story. God's Son addresses us not from a golden throne but out of the midst of the same life-stuff. He immerses himself in the Jordan, leaves footprints on the beach alongside fisherfolk, eats with publicans and sinners, bleeds amongst criminals and, according to tradition, lies dead in Joseph of Arimathea's garden tomb.

The Incarnation is a levelling out of absolute inequalities for the purposes of communication. Christ, says Paul, "though he was rich became poor so that by his poverty you might become rich". Or as Irenaeus put it, "He became what we are in order that we might become what he is." In the communications trade, this would be known as adjusting the frequencies so that voice and ear are on the same wavelength.

But self-disclosure involves all the risks of openness and vulnerability. Once the crustacean emerges from its shell, it is naked and at the mercy of predators. The proverb says that what we don't know can't hurt us. Possibly. But what *is* known about us can sometimes hurt very much.

If we come out from the shadows or from behind high walls, we make a much clearer target for those who wish us ill.

And if it is God who chooses to engage in self-disclosure, then he is the most inviting target of all. He who dwells in light unapproachable becomes the one who can be seen, heard and touched – and not all the hands laid upon him were loving and respectful.

This brings us to the Cross as the inevitable price of God's self-disclosure. On Calvary, God's heart is nakedly exposed – a reality which can be rejected or ignored but not misunderstood. It was perfect communication at infinite cost, epitomized in the technical term for Christ's saving work, atonement – personal relationship in total harmony without barrier or distance. And the proof text of atonement, "God was in Christ reconciling the world to himself", is an image of parties coming into perfect alignment, of the adjustment of wavelengths, of distortions being clarified.

Then again, a *system* of communication rather than a sporadic burst of messages passing hither and thither requires a network or grid with some degree of permanence. The Christian grid is called the communion of the Holy Spirit. In Bishop John V. Taylor's phrase, the gap between believers is bridged by the go-between God – the Holy Spirit powers the system. It provides the energy which enables Christians to be fully present to one another in self-disclosure. As at Pentecost, it is the Spirit which enables a wide variety of believers to find a common language. And the fruits of the Spirit – love, joy, peace, patience, kindness, goodness, faithfulness, gentleness and self-control – are precisely those human qualities which

18

permit self-disclosure without fear of exploitation or manipulation.

Finally, when the gap between the parties is not just bridged but transcended, then communication solidifies into communion. There is unity not just of meaning but of life. The New Testament points to the quality of this human togetherness in such images as Body, Church, People, Kingdom, Fellowship . . .

. . . and the New Israel. The name God gives to Jacob after the encounter at Peniel, **Israel**, is eventually extended to a whole people, a group of tribes whose common characteristic is that they are united in the worship of the one God, Yahweh. The Bible is properly agnostic about the detail of the virtually unimaginable condition where the Divine/human communication process is complete; when God has disclosed as much about himself as his creatures can bear. But it is a state described by terms such as *kabod* in the Old Testament and *doxa* in the New Testament: Glory.

Until the consummation, we shall continue to need theologies as communication systems – images and words which attempt to describe what believers have experienced when God discloses something of himself. Plato talked of shadows in a cave; Paul pointed to blurred reflections in a mirror; and Isaiah wrote of the "whisper of his ways" – as though God walked by us, and we knew he had passed only because the hem of his garment stirred the air.

In fact, that is not a bad description of Christian communication – the attempt to magnify the whisper of God's ways as he crosses the ford at the River Jabbok or walks through the sands of Galilee or enters a room silently at Emmaus to break bread with the disciples.

Sign of Contradiction

The gregarious God teases us with paradoxical behaviour. He moves towards us in self-disclosure, and yet we must wrestle with him to win from him what he chooses to reveal before he disengages from the encounter and retires into unfathomable mystery. And so we come up against the hard fact that in the last resort absolute clarity, perfect intelligibility and pure truth are beyond us, however thoroughly we master the communications trade; we are dealing in Mystery.

The God who blesses Jacob by endorsing their struggle as genuine personal encounter is also the God who slips away at dawn before he can be clearly seen in the morning sun. This illustrates the inevitable ambiguity of all religious communication — flashes of light in the darkness, divine advance and withdrawal, an elusive touch, the whisper of his ways.

In no translation of the Bible is Jacob's opponent clearly identified as God. One version reports that it was an angel; another, a man. The German Old Testament scholar Gerhard von Rad in his commentary on Genesis says that the word usually translated "man" in the account "is open to the widest possible interpretation".

Jacob believes himself to have been face to face with God at Peniel, but it *is* an act of faith. He will never know. Christian communication can never have that absolute clarity one might expect from a telephone directory or a railway timetable. Yet one thing on which all witnesses agree is that God's mystery is attractive rather than sinister. As Habbakuk put it, "His brightness was as the light, even though he hid his power".

The Gospel itself provides evidence of this ambiguity by the way it generates puzzlement, tension and conflict in any culture. How else is one to come to terms with one of the sterner of Christ's offices, Sign of Contradiction – "He is destined to be a sign which men reject. Many in Israel will stand and fall because of him" (Luke 2:34)? All Christian communicators face the challenge of Christ's terse deflation of their first-century counterparts "Tell no man!"

There is unfathomable mystery here. And mystery is a curious combination of knowledge and ignorance. If God were totally mysterious, there would be no disclosure, and we need not bother our heads about Christian communication at all. Contrariwise, were God to be completely intelligible, then theology could be transformed into a science, with the Almighty as its prize exhibit.

As it is, we hover uneasily between mystery and intelligibility. The problem of religious language illustrates the point. Take the perennial arguments about liturgical reform. Some radical reformers seek an accommodation with secular culture that would result in ritual language which is wholly contemporary but, according to their opponents, is too superficial to bear the weight of mystery.

On the other hand, the staunchest traditionalists seem to believe that mystery can be dissolved without remainder into sixteenth-century language. For them, the sonorous sentences of the ancient liturgies speak for themselves; even the ritual incantation in public worship of words with no contemporary meaning is thought to convey power. In so-called primitive societies, this would be regarded as magic.

Once religious experience is expressed in some language, whether of words, images or gestures, it loses its raw purity and inherits a history and a location. Every language has evolved over time and emerged from some social

21

setting that has determined its structure. The body of spiritual truth contained in the Koran has inevitably been shaped by the Arabic language and the region from which it came. Had Jesus been born in Africa rather than the Near East, the Gospel, both in style and structure, would presumably have reflected the notions of time and matter embodied in Bantu as opposed to Semitic languages. No doubt God took this into account when choosing the Jews.

If the ultimate raw material of religious communication is mystery, there is bound to be confusion, misunderstanding and pain in it. Hence, Christian communicators are likely to be recognizable not by the slickness of their tongue nor the sophistication of their equipment, but by an air of bafflement and a furrowed brow. They will also have a severed ham-string to show they have been wrestling with God like Jacob at Peniel.

The Tap on the Shoulder

Because God's gracious self-disclosure is bodied forth in history rather than merely bellowed forth in religious utterance, communication is not just a speech-event. According to the Bible, God teases all the human senses. Jacob discovered that. He not only argued with God and saw his outline vaguely in the darkness but also felt his heat, tasted his sweat and grappled with his body as he tried to throw him.

The patriach was not alone in this experience. God could be smelled in the smoke on Mount Horeb; heard by Elijah in the still, small voice; tasted and found gracious by the Psalmist; his garment's hem touched in Galilee; and seen in apparitions, visions and dreams, and finally disclosed in the light of the knowledge of the glory of God in the face of Jesus Christ.

Significantly, an early witness, the author of the First Letter of John, also testifies to the full sensuousness of the divine communication: "That which we have heard, which we have seen with our eyes, which we have looked upon, and touched with our hands, concerning the word of life" (1:1).

Note the word **touched**. Jacob got even closer than that. He didn't just touch God, he tried to get him in an arm-lock, throw him to the ground and knock him senseless. This suggests a rule about Christian communication likely to have the religious mass media industry in uproar. All forms of Christian communication other than face to face contact are in one way or another defective.

Jacob and the mysterious stranger did not harangue one another from opposite banks of the River Jabbok; they collided in close encounter. They laid hands on each other. Communication as self-disclosure means opening ourselves to whatever claims the other party chooses to make on us.

This is why face to face contact was the original method of spreading the Gospel. It is hard to think of more than a handful of instances where Jesus was beyond the reach of anyone who wished to tap him on the shoulder and ask him to make good the promises he offered in his sayings.

In the Bible, physical contact often communicates new life. "Behold, this has touched your lips; your guilt is taken away", one of the seraphim tells Isaiah; the Lord touches Jeremiah's lips to put words in his mouth; the sound Ezekiel hears as the glory of the Lord surrounds him is that of angel wings touching one another. Daniel sees a vision of the Lord and hears the sound of his words, but it is when a hand grasps his knee that he knows beyond doubt who is addressing him.

And the gospel record shows that it is often by the process of touching and being touched that Jesus communicates physical and spiritual wholeness. He risks ceremonial defilement to touch the leper; he squeezes the hand of Peter's sick mother-in-law; he lays his hand across the eyes of the two blind men, and touches the tongue of the deaf and dumb man at Decapolis – and so on and on.

But there is also the complementary power, a willingness to be touched. The sick men of Gennesaret and the woman with the haemorrhage reach out for the hem of his robe and are healed. The ministry of Jesus is a testimony to the efficacy and the cost of touching; tactile communication – that accessibility which allows men and women to lay hands on the Word of Life.

Is it an utterly outrageous thought that something quite fundamental went out of Christianity the first time an early apostle no longer needed to look an enquirer in the eye and say, "The man Jesus whom I follow has commanded me to love you as myself", and could instead say, "This is called a gospel. Read it!"? Possibly at that point a link in the chain of the apostolic succession snapped. Hundreds of people could read about Jesus at the same time; thousands heard the Gospel read aloud to them. Whole communities were baptized into the name of Jesus, and the cells of the Christian organism rapidly multiplied. The Church was well on its way to becoming a powerful institution, with branches throughout the known world.

And the minimal cost of discipleship was reduced. Or rather, the same amount of effort could be applied with greater efficiency. A hundred people could be reached through copies of a tract or epistle in less time than it took to deal with half-a-dozen enquirers who wanted to argue or belabour the apostles with their troubles.

That is an obvious parody of early church history. But my serious point is that the mechanization of the message by whatever means — through writing or print or electronic media — can preclude that embarrassing tap on the shoulder as a hearer responds to our proclamation of the Gospel with the demand, "Prove it!"

As Marshall McLuhan has reminded us, all techniques of mass communication are extensions of the human senses — print and camera are modelled on the eye, telephone and radio imitate the ear, and electronic devices ape the central nervous system. And by their aid it is possible to magnify the impact of the Gospel to an extent undreamed of by Jesus and the earliest Christians. There is, however, one crucial difference. It is speech without speaker, image without presence, contact without personal engagement. We may hear and see the Word of Life, but we cannot touch it.

By courtesy of the mass media, Christian communicators can tell the whole world about the love of God without it necessarily costing them any more than the expenditure of a little time and a lot of technique. It is love at a distance — at the other end of a microphone, camera or printing press. Those who speak of God's love through the mass media are often beyond the reach of the millions who would like to reach out and *touch* the Word of Life incarnate in the messenger. They cannot, because we who mediate it are locked away in studios, or behind desks in publishers' offices, or in the newsrooms of religious journals.

There are exceptions to most rules. In at least one instance known to me, a radio programme about religion liberated a young man who had been brought up in an atmosphere of suffocating piety. Face to face contact with a mother and father who were genuinely devout but spiritually tyrannical, far from making God's love real to him, had oppressed his spirit, stifled his mind and made him loathe religion. And it was a ghostly radio voice which gave him the stupendous news that God is not like *that*! But such a case of spiritual pathology does not undermine my general point.

If remoteness of the mass media is one hindrance to true communication, their spurious authority is another. In 1958, when I was a missionary in what was then Northern Rhodesia, the Government decreed that part of the Gwembe Valley should be flooded to enlarge Lake Kariba. The story goes that the Paramount Chief of the tribe in the Valley addressed his people and told them of the splendid new houses and gardens awaiting them on the high ground. The people murmured angrily, turned away and refused to move. A few days later, the Paramount Chief's appeal was broadcast from Radio Lusaka. The people heard it over the wireless and packed their bags without further protest.

Why? The Valley people did not think of the radio as some form of magic; they'd been accustomed to it for years. But there is compelling authority in the disembodied voice. Edmund Carpenter, the social anthropologist, noted the same phenomenon in a different cultural setting. "I knew a Californian who read his poetry out loud at parties until his friends learned to silence him. But when he played recordings of these same poems, everybody listened."

So people are disposed to listen to the remote, authoritative voice that addresses them on behalf of the Platonic God of the ether – a Being whose centre is everywhere and whose borders are nowhere. But is it the Spirit's leading or a subtle form of intimidation to invite the old, the lonely and the vulnerable to reach out for the untouchable through radio and television?

God's gracious act of self-disclosure is, as the hymn says, "interpreted by love", and real love, like cheap wine, does not travel well. It requires the living presence of the loving agent to express itself in its fullness. Presumably this is what made the Incarnation necessary — because God found loving at a distance frustrating.

If the one whose name and very nature is love felt the need to be corporeally present with his children in order to express love fully, what capacity have we, whose nature is flawed and our love faltering, to project it at a distance? We know from our own earth-bound experience the difference between love at a distance and the real thing. The most fulsome words of affection on a greetings card are a poor substitute for the attempt, however inadequate, to say the same thing face to face. A silent handshake may be more eloquent than a long speech of condolence.

Love needs no medium — no wires or gadgets or paper or print. It communicates itself. There is only one condition: bare presence, touchability. Of course, this may be impossible, and a voice over the telephone or a letter the best we can do. These substitutes are not to be despised. But they *are* substitutes. In the era of the mass media that much must be affirmed in the teeth of the stream of technological determinism that threatens to engulf us.

The Stumbling Block

In the epic struggle at Peniel, Jacob eventually prevailed at the point of greatest weakness, as his strength ebbed; he staggered away from the battlefield, maimed. In just the same way, the Gospel makes its appeal from earthly weakness to earthly strength; it is preached from the Cross to the secular powers.

This is a reversal of the dynamics of mass communication. The media are dominating influences, communicating from strength to weakness, power to impotence, huge conglomerate to frail human listener or viewer. Some theologians talk about the **impassibility** of God, by which they mean that he is incapable of suffering, injury or even emotion. The electronic media have their own pseudo-impassibility. It is customary to refer to radio and television *networks*, but they are more like conduits through which a single source addresses many outlets which are known with numbing accuracy as "receivers".

The mass media qualify as "principalities and powers" in the Pauline sense — secular institutions of vast potency operating under the sketchiest of outside control. They do not pretend to be democratic, and ordinary people have little access to them. Writes Gunther Anders, "When the world speaks to us without our being able to speak to it, we are deprived of speech and hence condemned to be unfree."

The Cross, in stark contrast, is the supreme example of non-dominating communication; indeed, it is communication by the dominated. Therefore, it is as Paul said, a "stumbling block" to Christians in the mass media who find themselves committed to an absurdity — proclaiming from positions of great secular power a Gospel which demonstrates the futility of secular power compared to the strength of God exhibited in utter weakness on the Cross. And it is when we collide with the supreme stumbling block of the Cross that we end up with a pronounced limp.

All this suggests a negative conclusion about the mass

media as suitable vehicles of Christian communication. That is not my intention. My concern is to challenge a certain euphoria amongst Christians, a tendency to get carried away by the drama and excitement generated by the electronic media – thus inducing an easy triumphalism about their religious possibilities which needs to be deflated.

Billy Graham has said, "Television is the most powerful tool of communication ever devised by man. Each of my prime-time special programmes is now carried by nearly three hundred stations across the U.S. and Canada. So that in a single broadcast I preach to more millions than Christ did in his lifetime."[1]

No doubt. But those millions cannot reach out to a television screen and *touch* the Word of Life. By all means we must master the media for God's sake. But it is proper to end by reminding you of that image of Jacob, a specific man in an individual encounter struggling to win clarity and understanding from darkness and mystery. This assuredly prefigures Jesus, the shocking particularity of whose love mocks *mass* media or mass *anything*, and who said, "I do not pray for the world. I pray for *these*".

TWO

THE LIBERTY
OF PROPHESYING

In 1647 Jeremy Taylor wrote *A Discourse of the Liberty
of Prophesying*. It was a compassionate and warmly chari-
table tract, written at a time of harsh religious controversy
and bitterness in the stormy middle years of the seven-
teenth century. I have borrowed Bishop Taylor's title for
this chapter, but from that point on, any resemblance
between what follows and his magisterial work is a
triumph of coincidence over competence.

It is a phrase that promises a dangerous and seductive
licence. Does the liberty of prophesying offer preachers
the freedom to say whatever happens to be occupying their
minds at the moment, to lay about them in the pulpit with
merry abandon, slaughtering sacred cows by the herd and,
in a crescendo of mixed metaphors, bringing down the
pillars of the temple around them – to the alarm, fury or
excitement of their hearers?

Undoubtedly, the supreme compliment the contemporary Church can pay a man (and I use the word "man"
advisedly – female prophets tend to be written off as
feminist scolds) is neither to wrap episcopal gaiters round
his legs nor a doctoral hood round his neck, but to attach
that magic adjective "prophetic" to his name. Then he
becomes the darling of the students and the bane of their
professors. His lightest word is treated as holy writ, and

the adulation he receives from radicals is only equalled by the degree of suspicion he arouses in all Establishments, political and ecclesiastical.

There *are* men and women in the modern Church, and outside it, who self-evidently share the same vocation as those Hebrew wild men of the Old Testament. They see things steadily and see them whole, whilst the rest of us thrash around treating the world like a cheap watch – to be subjected to inexpert investigation until all the pieces lie in front of us, defying our efforts to put them together again.

And these choice spirits do seem to enjoy liberty in prophesying – they are their own men or women. Their minds are not trapped in the ruts of unthinking orthodoxy; they jump to no party whip nor do they dance to anyone else's tune. They do not hold a wet finger up to the wind before they express an opinion, nor do they bother over-much either about applause or vilification.

Yet true prophets are not iconoclasts who, like Cromwell's soldiers rampaging through the monasteries, have a thoroughly enjoyable time smashing sacred things. Though they may show a seeming irreverence towards earthly authority, they are always conscious of being accountable to a higher tribunal. There is a gravitas about their style and speech which is a universe away from mere mischief-making.

These major contemporary prophets are a law unto themselves. Their specific genius seems unique and inimitable. And yet, according to the Bible, that wry wish of Moses recorded in The Book of Numbers, "Would that *all* the Lord's people were prophets!", was granted a long time later at Pentecost where "*All* present were filled with the Spirit and began to speak. . . ." So it is equally erroneous to regard prophecy as the monopoly of a few titans, or as the trade of any old pulpit-ranter who believes that the outrageous ideas he imposes upon God's people are proved true by the amount of shock and outrage they evoke.

The word "prophet" is obviously in need of some rehabilitation. Let us try to get back to first principles, and that means studying the Hebrew prophets – which is a restricted field. We are referring to at most fifteen or twenty men who appeared in Israel over a period of five or six centuries. Indeed, so carefully did God ration the supply to one prophet per generation, that when two or three coincided in time, another generation went without their prophet.

The Bible as Crystal Ball

Before we can get a clear look at the Hebrew prophets, it is necessary to get rid of the popular misconception that they were fortune tellers able to stare across the hills of eighth-century Judaea and see the rise of modern China or the splitting of the atom. And this in turn means rejecting any notion that the book which records their words can be treated as a crystal ball. Yet throughout the Christian centuries the Bible has been described as a work of prophecy. What can that mean?

Alarm bells ring all round our skulls whenever anyone talks about the Bible as a work of prophecy. We have been ensnared in too many ill-tempered arguments with Jehovah's Witnesses and other self-appointed Keepers of the Oracle. We have blushed with embarrassment for the honour of the Hebrew prophets as their more enigmatic utterances have been taken, twisted and offered as long-foreshadowed solutions to complex issues that baffle the best minds of our day.

Our heads reel at the dogged reiteration of the circular argument that the Bible is true because many of the prophecies it contains have come true and therefore the prophecies which have not yet been fulfilled assuredly will be, because the Bible is true. The error is the more monstrous because in a certain sense the argument is sound. There is only a hair's-breadth difference in the phraseology used by the serious student of the Bible and the literalist who states the same truth, but there is a gap of many centuries in understanding.

Scientific biblical criticism rang down the curtain on a splendidly colourful era stretching from the primitive Church to the nineteenth century, during which the vindication of the Bible as a record of miraculous predictions, the argument from prophecy, was a powerful theme in Christian preaching and apologetic.[2]

Literalism, the reading forward of biblical predictions to their fulfilment, and allegory, the reading back into prophetic writings meanings their authors could not have intended, were the twin lenses through which Holy Scripture was scanned to search out prophecy. And strangely beautiful and moving were some of these allegorical interpretations of books like the Song of Songs out of the mouths of master-preachers of the time.

The argument from prophecy was used by great doctors of the Church, from Augustine through Aquinas to Luther, with a power and subtlety not evident in the crude literalism of some modern biblical soothsayers. Nor did they mistake a fevered imagination for prophetic illumination; hence, Augustine's insistence that you had better be sure any fancy interpretation you put on a biblical passage is spoken of plainly elsewhere in Scripture.

And one is awed by the unrelenting single-mindedness of Martin Luther in demanding that all biblical prophecy must be read as pointing to and interpreted in the light of Jesus Christ. So rigorously did he apply this rule that he claimed to read into one tiny word of the first commandment – "You shall love the Lord *your* God" – the whole scheme of salvation through Christ. Thus, he controls prophecy by the simple expedient of making sure that even when it is wrong it speaks of Christ.

Of course, a cynic might echo the words of Horace Walpole, "The wisest prophets make sure of events first!", as he observed the puncturing of the prophetic afflatus by the sharp needle of biblical criticism. Careful scholarship made the Old Testament prophets seem like conjurors caught stuffing rabbits into hats when the theatre curtain rises prematurely. Isaiah's realized prediction that the Jews would be freed from captivity during the reign of King Cyrus a hundred years hence was highly impressive. Then probing scholars detected the work of a Second Isaiah interwoven with that of the First and writing as a contemporary of Cyrus. Daniel's colourful soothsayings become a little pallid when his book is re-dated to reveal him writing of past events and not future expectations. And so on and on.

What in fact modern biblical scholarship has done is to humanize the Old Testament prophets. No longer do they stand on the stage of history as mindless megaphones, booming words broadcast from a transmitting station beyond the stars. They were men of their time, immersed in events and sometimes magnificently wrong in their estimate of the drift of things.

We revere them not for their ability to divine the future but for their perspicacity in detecting in the events of their time the shifting elusive pattern of history as a whole, broken and enigmatic and yet deriving such unity as it possesses from God's sovereignty over it.

We do not assign greatness to a Jeremiah and an Isaiah because they had the percipience to predict the rise of modern Russia or the invention of the nuclear bomb. They did something much more impressive. They traced those forces operating in the human heart and human society which in every time will create and destroy great powers and elevate the misuse of human knowledge to the level of the demonic. They addressed their own age and yet spoke to the total human condition.

Only when the Bible as Crystal Ball is smashed is there revealed beneath the rubble a mosaic whose pattern is the ground-plan of salvation. The whole of the Old Testament and not just the sayings of the prophets is seen to be prophetic, pointing forward beyond itself. A dimension in every event recorded in it offers a clue to the shape and goal of all history.

To go any further along this tack is to take us into the New Testament, for as the apostles recognized, Jesus is the clue to the Old Testament; looking back from him we can see what the leading of the divine purpose was. But I want to stick with the rugged prophets of the old Israel, these men whose minds were hospitable to thoughts about God, indeed, open to the persuasions of God to a degree their contemporaries thought foolish or fanatical or plain wrong.

Before the First World War, the American President Woodrow Wilson said this about what he called the new radicalism in politics: "It consists not in the things proposed but in the things disclosed." That is as neat a definition of prophecy as one would find, chiming in well with the often-quoted phrase to the effect that the Hebrew prophets were forth-tellers rather than foretellers. What, then, have they to teach Christian communicators? What were the distinctive features of the prophetic style?

A Public Ministry

Paul said in his speech before Agrippa: "This thing was not done in a corner" (Acts 26:26). Neither Judaism nor Christianity are mystery religions, trading in secrets, dabbling in esoteric knowledge, their ambit confined to dark and private places from which unbelievers are excluded.

Priests by nature and training tend to be guardians of holy things and sacred places, of correctly performed rituals and cherished traditions. Prophets, on the other hand, are committed to a public ministry. Whilst the priest whispers in the sanctuary, the prophet bellows in the market place.

And the prophets have the best of the argument, for Christ was not sacrificed on some ritual Temple altar in holy silence but, as the Epistle to the Hebrews said, crucified outside the city gate on a public holiday. Our salvation, as Paul pointed out to Agrippa, was not accomplished behind closed doors; we who follow Christ are condemned to be public spectacles, living out and accomplishing our destiny before the whole world (1 Corinthians 4:9).

The public nature of the prophetic ministry cannot be over-emphasized at a time when the age-old arguments about the Church keeping out of politics are being rehearsed with great stridency. Politics is concerned with the affairs of the "polis" – the organized community. And

that is where the prophet is to be found. The priest minds
his own business, which is tending the temple and the
altar. The prophet has no business of his own; the world
is his business.

Inevitably, much Old Testament prophecy was taken up
with what we would now call political issues. This is not
necessarily because the prophets were by temperament and
cast of mind the kind of people who in the twentieth
century would be standing for Parliament rather than
acting as spokesmen for the Lord. Rather, it was because
they were, as God told Ezekiel, watchmen by divine
appointment over a nation always under threat in a hostile
environment.

Those of a priestly mind-set tend to interpret history in
such a way as to give most weight to those movements
and personalities who have left behind some ecclesiastical
residue – a creed, a sect or a church. It was, I think,
Harvey Cox, the American theologian, who pointed out
that we give a hundred pages to Martin Luther for every
page devoted to Thomas Munzer, the sixteenth-century
German Anabaptist and political rebel. Yet the sociologist
Karl Mannheim claims that the social revolutions of the
sixteenth century, of which Munzer was a leader, un-
leashed tides that still flow through the contemporary
world. But Luther gets all the attention because he founded
a church and a religious movement bearing his name.

So, too, the Puritans. The fact that they founded
churches outweighs the significance of their discovery of
the politics of participatory democracy – Cromwell's
enemies sneered because in his Puritan army even tinkers
and cobblers were allowed to take part in political discussion and action. And the often-quoted remark of the
late General Secretary of the Labour Party, Morgan Phil-

lips, that the British Labour Party owes more to Methodism than Marxism, is usually a footnote to a highly ecclesiastical interpretation of Wesley's impact upon Britain.

The landmarks of Hebrew history which the prophets recalled again and again were not ecclesiastical – at least, not in the pious sense of that robustly secular Old Testament word – but political events: exodus, conquest, exile, captivity and the end of the Kingdom. "What is God saying to us through this upheaval?", was the question which preoccupied them.

And they had not the priestly propensity for making nice distinctions between religious observance and political obedience. The prophets were the guardians of the Covenant, or "Treaty" – could you have a more political term? They summoned the people to responsible stewardship of all that God had given, and reminded them of what he demanded in return. This was politics in the grand sense – the affairs of the *polis* as the realm where human beings gain dignity and freedom on God's terms or are at the mercy of forces which rob them of their essential humanity.

It is characteristic of the public ministry of the prophets that they were less fastidious in their choice of allies than priests would have been. Whilst priests insisted that only true believers, ritually clean and of impeccable spiritual pedigree, could be the instruments of God's will, the prophets were less choosy. Their reading of events led them to the conclusion that to get his work done, God was willing to use those who denied him, did not know him or even defied him.

Calvin has a majestic passage in *The Institutes* in which he expounds this prophetic reading of history:

Thus God tamed the pride of Tyre by the Egyptians; the insolence of the Egyptians by the Assyrians; the ferocity of the Assyrians by the Chaldeans; the confidence of Babylon by the Medes and Persians. All these things were not done in the same way, though they were directed by the hand of God, as seemed to him good, and did his work without knowing it.

However, in their willingness to find allies where they were able, the prophets did not go too far and fall into the trap of assuming that any ally was a true believer who had just not woken up to the fact. Cyrus the pagan king was, according to Isaiah, the rod of God's anger, the agent of his purposes, but that did not place him amongst the blessed. He could not receive the covenant promise of a God in whom he did not believe. The prophets were always able to distinguish between God's providence and his favour.

This is an essentially political way of looking at things. Politics draws people into temporary and limited alliances without assuming they share the same ultimate values. Hence, the prophets could locate a specific political event in God's scheme of things without reading either too much or too little into it.

There was a precision about prophetic utterances; they were not abstract statements of general principle but applied to one time and place. They were spoken at a particular moment in Israel's history, and it was necessary to know the history in order to understand the prophecy.

Unlike the priestly word, which may be passed down from generation to generation virtually unchanged, the prophetic word is spoken in a form adapted to the contemporary situation and may be pointless in any other. For prophecy is a moral indictment intended to bring about real change there and then. Once the words are preserved beyond the time to which they are addressed, they harden into dogma. For is not dogma the corpse of dead prophecy?

A Traditional Ministry
There is a popular idea that prophets appeared on the landscape of Israel almost like figures from another planet, or as what are called in the breeding world "sports", exotic and inexplicable variations from the norm. Yet the Hebrew prophets did not lay about them in public with the happy abandon of those without any prior loyalties or obligations – free to say whatever came into their head because they were bound by no rules nor required to stick to any agreed text.

In fact, the prophets were the product of a long period of trial and error. The prophetic tradition in Israel had been a long time coming to flower. The wild dervishes of an earlier period had given way to fortune tellers who were less extreme in their behaviour though as eccentric in their ideas; then the fortune tellers become foretellers more concerned with the future of the nation than with the fate of private clients. Reckless prediction was superseded by strong moralizing as foretellers evolved into preachers. The prophetic faculty slowly moved over the generations from the fevered brain of the ecstatics, the *Nebi'im*, to the sensitive conscience of the pre-exilic prophets.

Thus did the institution of prophecy undergo a constant process of refinement. Amos, for example, was in some ways a point of departure and his genius could not be traced back to any obvious predecessor. He was a graduate of no known school of prophecy, having spent his days on the fringes of the desert around Tekoa. Yet his choice of the nomadic life as a conscious rejection of the luxury and religiosity of the northern kingdom was not a radical new departure but a desire to return to the days of wilderness religion.

Jeremiah also appeals to the tradition — "I gave your ancestors no commands about burnt-offerings or other kinds of sacrifices when I brought them out of Egypt" (7:22). And Hosea and Micah hark back to the simple, austere religion of the desert — those wilderness days which were the time of Israel's golden youth, when the test of true religion was the way the poor were treated.

The prophetic spirit therefore is not characterized by novelty and complete originality of thought. Prophets were not in the business of founding a new religion but of calling people back to the primitive purity of the old one. They were never theologically fancy free, plucking diverting notions about God out of thin air and hoping to start a fashion. When they parted company from their co-religionists it was with deep regret and not adolescent glee. In the same way, their passionate impatience was an expression of slowly maturing conviction and not momentary irritation. They were angry men, not irascible ones.

The prophetic call to the people to change their ways came not out of a rejection of tradition but from a sense that its possibilities had been fulfilled or else exhausted. Only from the jumping off point of the old way do prophets launch themselves in new directions. The church door at Luther's Wittenberg may have been a point of departure; it was also an arrival point. The Reformation saw the resolution of issues that had been coming to a head for generations.

There are morals for us here. There is a tendency in the contemporary Church to identify prophecy with iconoclasm, as though the act of putting a foot through the stained glass window is by definition a blow for God's truth, and to love the Church or have any lingering loyalty to it is evidence of weakness and lack of prophetic will.

Nothing less than a scorched earth policy will do. Only through the burnt and blackened stubble of the old vegetation can the fresh green shoots of the new crop force their way into the light. The dictum of theologian, Paul Tillich, is the rallying cry. He wrote, "The new is not created out of the old, not out of the best of the old, but out of the death of the old". That's the thing! Put the rachitic old faith, with its rheumy eyes and shaking hands and wheezy breathing, out of its misery. Drive it out into the freezing night, as the Eskimos used to do with their geriatric relatives.

Emerson said that he loved Nay-sayers more than Yea-sayers. We all have some admiration for awkward customers who are not prepared to be subservient to the conventional wisdom, or bow the knee to Baal because everyone else does. Prophets are usually regarded as Nay-sayers who might be expected to dissent from conventional religious propositions. Yet the Nay-sayer does not speak out of a vacuum, but in reaction to somebody's Yea. Only against a framework of affirmations do denials make any sense. The black mass requires the eucharist, and Anti-Christ could have no identity unless measured against the Son of God. So, too, Death of God theology is meaningless except in reaction against Christian orthodoxy – society at large has been insisting for a long time that there is no God; the scandal of the "God is Dead" school is that these are Christian theologians and not militant atheists who have been making the claim — Nay-saying from the heart of Yea-saying territory.

So true prophets as Nay-sayers take tradition, the preserve of the Yea-sayers, with the utmost seriousness. Far from parting company from their orthodox comrades in the faith in a captious spirit, like that of naughty schoolboys tearing up their exercise books, they do so with sadness and the gravest of misgivings. The tradition is a precious heritage to them. Just as the Hebrew prophets claimed kinship with those mighty patriarchs, Abraham, Isaac and Jacob, so the Christian tradition, stretching back to the apostles and including along the way intellectual and spiritual giants, is not to be brushed aside carelessly. To turn one's back on what the Reformers called "Scripture and the Fathers" is no light thing.

The tradition is a datum-point like a landmark in the desert, so the prophet who launches himself bravely into the unknown can always find his way back if he gets hopelessly lost. Thus, some of God's greatest servants who felt impelled to strike out into the dark have still kept one eye on the lights of home twinkling behind them. To the end of his life Martin Luther always referred to the Church of Rome from which he had parted company as his "Holy Mother", and John Wesley insisted throughout the schism that he was a loyal son of the Church of England. All the while Dietrich Bonhoeffer, in a Nazi prison, was claiming that the whole of traditional Christianity must go into the melting pot, he was nerving himself for his ultimate ordeal at the hands of the executioner on a diet of Reformation hymns and traditional prayers.

Even the most radical prophet recognizes that there are turbulent times when it is the very rigidity of a conservative faith that holds things together. As G. K. Chesterton pointed out in *Orthodoxy*:

> Religion is a very terrible thing, truly a raging fire; and Authority is often quite as much needed to restrain it as to impose it . . . . Creed and dogma have saved the sanity of the world. If in the really Dark Ages there had been a religion of feeling, it would have been a religion of black and suicidal feeling. It was a rigid creed that resisted the rush of suicidal feeling.

Prophets therefore are not anarchists but radicals. As the word implies, they desire to get to the root of the matter, to be rid of the accumulated clutter and irrelevance that have obscured the primitive faith. They are not invaders trying to reduce Jerusalem from the outside, but loyal citizens weeping over its state from its very heart. They are radical in two senses — in their desire to get back and down to the very roots of faith, and also in their firm rooting within that faith. Only because of their solid grounding in belief have they the security to question, to doubt, to challenge. Contrary to the popular meaning of the term, prophets are the real traditionalists. They are jealous for the truth — the core-meaning of the tradition which they believe successive generations and luke-warm believers have corrupted.

A Lay Ministry

With the exception of Ezekiel, the great Old Testament prophets were laymen, and their targets were often the priests who protected the vested interests of shrines, temples and soothsaying. There are biblical references to "schools of prophets" in Israel, but it is clear that these were not reputable theological colleges or seminaries, and the authentic prophets kept well clear of them. The moral indignation that runs throughout the history of the Judaeo-Christian religion is as much a layman's indictment of the complacency or outright corruption of the religious professionals as of the cupidity of the secular powers.

Amos gloried in his amateur status – "I was no prophet, neither was I a prophet's son: but I was a herdsman, and a gatherer of sycamore fruit; and the Lord took me as I tended the flock." He learned his trade in a rugged and often hostile environment, alone in the wilderness, caught up in the vagaries of nature. It was a physical setting which fired his mind to shape those vivid prophetic images he later used to such powerful effect – justice flowing like a stream and righteousness like a river that never goes dry, of locusts ravaging the green shoots and fire scorching the earth, and a man running from a lion and meeting a bear.

The glory of the heavens, the terrifying power of the storm, the perspective of the rocky heights from which Amos surveyed Israel, Judah, Edom and Moab gave him a sense of the majesty of God and the dwarfing of all human life in comparison to it – a quaint way of getting a theological education but hardly to be compared with a decent degree in divinity, as the priests would no doubt point out condescendingly.

Indeed, even if the historical evidence didn't reveal that the Hebrew prophets were laymen, the diffuse and unorganized nature of their writings would make us suspect that they had not received the benefits of a good theological college education. The clergy would have been much more systematic and measured in their utterances. As it is, the prophetic writings in the Old Testament are scattered from Genesis to Malachi, always fragmentary and sometimes plain contradictory. An untidy mess. Just what happens when untrained minds are let loose on the preserve of the professionals.

Prophecy is bound to be primarily a lay vocation for a very practical, even mercenary, reason. It sits ill with the clergy to thunder from the pulpit on Sundays about the evils of the acquisitive society and then the next day go into negotiation about stipend increases. Nor is it easy to call down the judgement of God on organized religion's smugness, inertia and worldliness whilst being paid to organize it. The professional's relationship to the people of God is ambiguous because what was intended to be his love has perforce to become his business. The hand raised one day in prophetic anathema against the religious institution is stretched out the next day to receive its dole.

That is not the fault of the professional clergy. Blame it on the fact that the Second Coming didn't come, the world didn't end on schedule as the early Christians were led to believe, and so an apocalyptic fellowship became an institution. And like all institutions in a fallen world, the Church succumbed to the laws of economics.

Amos fitted the identi-kit picture of the free-lance perfectly. Even had the religious institution gone up in flames as a result of his fiery verbal darts, nothing central to his survival was at stake. There would always be sycamore fruit salad and leg of mutton for supper – home grown, hand nurtured and entirely the product of his own industry.

The raw truth is that the religious professional who strives to be a prophet is virtually forced to live a double life. His scalding utterance is aimed at the heart of an institution which has undertaken to support him and his family and is entitled to receive from him in return at least a modicum of loyalty. Put more pictorially, the ecclesiasti-

cal prophet is busily engaged sawing off the very branch
of the tree on which he is perched. Pruning, cutting back
the wilder foliage is one thing, but root and branch extir-
pation as recommended by the Hebrew prophets would
leave him suspended in mid-air.

This is a riddle without a resolution, and the paid
employee of the Church who aspires to be a prophet must
live with the contradiction as best he can. The dilemma
may be so acute that he is forced to wrestle with the
proposition that possibly God is calling him to be a
layman. The days of the one-way call to the ministry are
long gone. The priestly notion that the man who lays aside
his clerical robes for street mufti is betraying some sacred
trust ignores the truth that ordination is a calling, not a
profession. After all, the first deacons were set apart by
the laying on of hands, not to celebrate high mass but to
wait on tables (Acts 6:1–6).

Yet there is a much more positive reason why prophecy
operates best as a lay vocation. The starting point for lay
theology is the world, for that is where lay people live,
move and have their being. The natural focus of their
thinking is not on liturgics or systematic theology or
ecclesiastical history or even the politics and gossip of
church assemblies, but on the pressure points of their lives.
And the pressure points of their lives have to do with such
things as attitudes to money, ambition, sex, and power —
themes high on the prophetic agenda.

Such a lay theology will tend to be unsystematic and as
specific as the statements of the Hebrew prophets. And
why not? Much technical theology is sweeping in its scope
and remote from the realities of life. It was Søren Kierke-
gaard who complained that when he asked Hegel for direc-

tions to a street address in Copenhagen he was given a map of Europe.

Since the laity are up past their necks in the world, it is the inevitable starting point for their thinking about God. True lay religion is not a form of experience separate from other forms of experience, but it is about the transform- ation of all experience, and particularly that bit they are immersed in. Discerning the meaning of events is the stuff of daily life; that's how we make sense of things. And this is the task of prophecy — discovering God's promise and judgement within a specific situation at a given time.

The priestly view of religion cannot free believers to concentrate on the present, for the cultic position is that only by incorporating them into a sacred past can they make sense of the present or take possession of the future. And to an extent that is true, since the redemptive work of Christ is final, fixed and was totally accomplished "under Pontius Pilate" — a long time ago.

So it is, I suppose, a matter of emphasis. Gibson Winter well summarizes the three classic styles of Christian pro- clamation — **priestly proclamation** incorporates believers into a restored creation; **evangelical proclamation** lifts them to a present state of redemption; and **prophetic proc- lamation** opens them to a future which they are empow- ered to create. All three have biblical warrant and cannot be mutually exclusive.[3]

Long centuries after God called lay prophets to do his work and Jesus and Paul were both prepared to trust their message to theologically untrained apostles, the modern Church now widely acknowledges that theology cannot be the exclusive preserve of experts. As the late and much lamented Bishop John Robinson wrote, "The current renewal of the Church in our day is marked not only by the biblical, liturgical and ecumenical movements but by that great quickening of the laity, a thawing of God's frozen people."

A Passionate Ministry

Not the happiest word – passionate. But I know of no other which says quite what I mean. Consider Jeremiah's account of his call. The King James Version found the original metaphor the prophet himself used a little strong, and so substituted the English word "deceived" for the Hebrew word "seduced": *O Lord, you have seduced me, and I was seduced: you are stronger than I am and prevailed.* To put it plainly, Jeremiah was swept off his feet and ravished. The prophet was press-ganged. He was not just chosen, but overwhelmed. He wasn't a natural talker with a yen to hear the sound of his own voice. He pleaded inexperience, ignorance, youth and a history of failure. To no avail. His resistance was overcome by the divine aggression.

The truly prophetic utterance has the quality of being forced upon someone. Things which could quite easily be left unsaid, that are the result of considered thought and careful decision, are no part of prophecy. We are not the masters of prophetic words; they master us. Luther, before the Diet of Worms, put it in a single sentence, "Ich kan nicht anders" – "I cannot do otherwise."

Words of prophecy well up out of a moral passion which can no longer be contained. Yet they emanate from a source deeper than bad temper or heated dissent. They are like a volcanic eruption, bursting out in fire and flame on the specific occasion. Were they to become chronic, habitual, a general style of utterance, they would cease to be prophetic. This is surely why the recorded words of the historic prophets are so fragmentary and precisely targeted. They are spoken out of a sense of overpowering necessity. It is there and then, or never.

Just as you cannot breed a prophet – he happens – so you cannot by linguistic or theological analysis trace a prophetic outburst. To ask where Jeremiah got his sermon in the temple from, or how Amos derived the searing condemnations at Bethel that had Amaziah begging him to go back to Judah, is like enquiring where Mozart got the C Minor Mass from. There is the mysterious quality of the given about all truly inspired utterances.

You can listen carefully for the echo of other voices in the prophet's speech, imagine the sources of his material, locate the formative influences on his thinking – but these are all dry bones. It is that breath from beyond that stirs them into life. And who knows when and from where it comes? As Jesus said, "The Spirit comes and goes as it chooses".

If the inspiration can be located anywhere, it is in the feeling with which the prophet imbues his words, provided of course those words are true. After all, words are just words. God didn't equip the prophets with a special vocabulary throbbing with unearthly power – otherwise, how could the prophets make themselves understood to the generality of the people? What, then, was the energizing centre of prophetic utterance? The great American preacher, Phillips Brooks, said that he who lacks emotion lacks expression. Prophetic words are shaped in the crucible of emotion; the two go together.

Any attempt in the pulpit to inject emotion into words formed in a spirit of cool deliberation in the study is an example of what has been called "spiritual unchastity". It is possible to forgive a preacher virtually anything, from faulty theology to faltering grammar, but not simulated emotion. They were not crocodile tears Christ shed over Jerusalem, and that sweat in Gethsemane which dripped on the ground like great drops of blood could not be squeezed out by play-acting, however inspired.

Some of the outstanding preachers of the Victorian era were often compared to great actors of the time. In manner, gestures, presence and dramatic sense, possibly. But if the intense emotion they conveyed was scripted along with the words, then they were frauds. Possibly the odd one was, but the evidence is that most were mightily used by God, and though he often recruited some very strange characters, ham actors were not amongst them.

Human emotions have their own integrity. So long as they are not meddled with or cynically manipulated, they will respond appropriately to whatever power or force moves them. But there is an equation in the business. It is, I think, the second law of thermodynamics which says you cannot get more out of something than you put in, and that includes the relationship between words and feelings. It is only possible to transmit through publicly uttered words the same amount of feeling as went into their preparation; any surplus is phoney.

It is this explosive mixture of emotion and words that explains the moral absoluteness of the prophets' utterance. There is none of the "nicely calculated less or more" about their reasoning. Their judgements have a crudity which would make any self-respecting scholar wince — no qualifications or balanced statements or carefully weighed arguments. Paul was squarely within the tradition when he told the Ephesians flatly, "*Your nation is separated from Christ, alienated from the commonwealth of Israel, a stranger to the covenant of promise, having no hope and*

51

without God in the world". What, every single living one
of them? Probably not, but prophets in full flood can't be
bothered with the small print.

The prophets are at their most imperious when calling
down the wrath of God on the nation. Prophecy's theme
is always righteousness and not theological orthodoxy, for
the determination of sound doctrine demands discussion
and reflection, and the prophets have no time for all that.
They know instantaneously when God's law is being viol-
ated in the life of the nation, almost by a gut instinct.
They feel it in their bowels, and they cry out as though in
pain, for what is an affront to God is like a sword thrust
at their vitals.

Prophets are not in the business of telling the people
how to get from their present parlous plight to a state of
blessedness, except in the broadest possible terms. They
demand repentance, and paint glowing pictures of the
Messianic order when the parched ground shall become a
pool and the thirsty land springs of water. They foresee
the day when the lion will lie down with the lamb and the
sucking child will play with the poisonous snake. But they
make no attempt to bridge the gap by proposing detailed
strategies and programmes of action.

Precisely how the sinful present is to be transformed
into a glorious future is a matter on which prophets are
silent. And no doubt, when pressed for their practical
proposals they would say much the same thing as Jesus
did when asked to intervene in a property dispute, "My
friend, who gave me the right to judge between
you . . . Guard yourself from every kind of greed." That
is not a very helpful response to a specific problem of
ethics but, in true prophetic style, it draws attention to a
moral absolute.

It is interesting to note how unconvincing prophets sound when they desert the moral high ground and try to make working connections between the ultimate ideal and the immediate situation. Thus, Ezekiel in full spate about the valley of dry bones and God's flock gathered by the Davidic shepherd onto good pasture is instinct with power and eloquence. Then, in a crashing anti-climax, he goes on to describe in detail the dimensions of the restored temple, its kitchen furnishings, its fireplaces against the wall and the vats where the sacrifices are to be boiled. And we know that we are off prophetic ground; this is Ezekiel the priest talking.

Now, in all fairness, somebody has to take care of the mechanics of running the temple and overseeing the economy of organized religion. But that isn't the prophet. He has one massive, overpowering preoccupation: confronting the nation with God, bringing the people back again and again to their primary engagement with the Lord of Hosts. Everything else is someone else's business. This is why prophecy is a passionate ministry. It can only be exercised by a God-obsessed, utterly single-minded man or woman.

Testing the Spirits

When we move into the world of the New Testament, the prophet is still to be found in the ranks of the early Church, but he seems to have lost that lonely dominance which characterized his eighth-century forebears. He now rubs shoulders with a whole gaggle of Christians exercising a variety of functions – as apostles, evangelists, pastors and teachers. His authority, too, seems less absolute in an organization that boasts deacons, presbyters and bishops. Unlike the empty hills of Tekoa, it's a busy world where the apostles bustle about doing many different things in the service of the Kingdom.

Whilst the importance of the prophetic office is affirmed in the New Testament, it has lost not only its uniqueness as the agency of God's word but is also subject to much closer scrutiny. The Old Testament prophets often got their facts wrong; things didn't happen as they said they would; but no one thought the worse of them on that account. They had spoken for God, that was the important thing. In the early Church, however, it wasn't enough to claim to be a prophet, one had to prove it. The prophet was heard, his words were weighed and put to the test, as much by his fellow prophets as by the generality of the believers. There was resolute self-criticism in the prophetic community – as Paul told the church at Corinth, "The spirits of the prophets are subject to the prophets". There was a holy self-discipline about them; almost the development of a professional ethic.

There are two reasons for this wary assessment of prophetic utterance. The first, of course, is that *the* prophecy had been fulfilled, the Christ had come as foretold in Scripture, so there was an absolute bench-mark by which prophetic authenticity could be assessed. Was it consonant with the spirit of Christ? Did it illuminate his life and teaching?

The other reason why prophets were put to the test presumably had to do with the fact that, unlike their Old Testament forebears who were lonely figures, they were part of a vibrant community in the early morning of its bright new life, bursting with the Spirit and probably exhibiting some of the symptoms of over-excitement as well. A narrow dividing line can sometimes separate rapture from hysteria; there are more ways than one of being carried away in the exhilaration of the moment.

Paul himself shows rare insight in this matter. He is always careful to distinguish between those times when he is declaring the word of the Lord, and those where he is stating his private opinions. When he ventures a comment "by permission and not of commandment" he is making a distinction shared also by the occupant of the papal throne whose utterances *ex cathedra* have a different status from any others he may make.

This is not a form of discrimination favoured by the Hebrew prophets. They had a degree of self-assurance that sometimes bordered on the arrogant. Ezekiel, for instance, gives no hint that his Valley of Dry Bones utterance had a different weight of authority from his rather tedious cataloguing of the contents of the temple. God giving new life to the spiritually moribund and the number of bricks in the temple wall were both filed under the same heading. One is reminded of the Baghdad street vendor's cry, "In the name of Allah! Figs".

How, then, did the early Church put prophetic speech to the test? The oldest and most reliable test was that proposed by Jesus who said, "By their fruits shall you know them" – the prophet's character should be in conformity with his words. God-thoughts that pass through the mind and fall off the lips yet leave no impress on character are highly suspect. Though religion and morality are not synonymous, it is a fair assumption that any true religious insight ought to result in a deepening of personal morality. The manifestations of religion may be vague, whereas those of morality are usually clear-cut. It is not always easy to judge whether someone has grown in piety and humility, but it is usually apparent whether he is honest and truthful.

The difficulty of course is that the test by moral character takes time. The fruits of which Jesus speaks may appear on the branches only after a prolonged period of growth. There are some prophets who seem to be awarded an instant recognition which is never subsequently withdrawn. St Francis of Assisi is an obvious case. Others never achieve acknowledgement until long after the event. So what is the Church to do in the interim? The Pauline answer was that the Church should use its common sense.

The early Christian communities numbered some very odd characters and sometimes did some very strange things. They were far from perfect human beings pledged to an absolute ideal, and though they sometimes fell from grace, they were still part of a grace-filled fellowship — charity recognizably shone through their shortcomings. Paul, therefore, was content to trust their honest good sense to test the spirits to see whether they were of God.

This is one of the crucial distinctions between Old Testament and New Testament prophets. The Hebrew prophets were indomitably solitary, almost self-entire in their convictions, conscious of answering only to God himself for their words. The prophetic ministry from New Testament times onwards has been exercised within a framework of corporate discipline. It cannot be accidental that the Christian communion which puts greatest store on the authority of the Inner Light, the Society of Friends, is also the one which appeals constantly to "the sense of the meeting" to verify the individual inspirations of its members.

The ultimate test of prophecy is the willingness to suffer for the right to speak it. In this way the prophet becomes a witness "unto blood". Laying one's life on the line is impressive testimony, yet the early Church seemed to exercise a wary caution about martyrdom, as though recognizing that even suffering is not necessarily self-authenticating. Christians may have to accept martyrdom, but they are not called to go out of their way looking for crosses on which to impale themselves.

There is an absolutism about the words spoken by those courting stern reprisals that silences all criticism. But it is necessary to comment that even spelling out prophetic words in one's own blood does not of itself guarantee their truth, though it commands the admiration and respect of more timorous believers.

The testing of the spirits remains the same, whether the prophet speaks from a pulpit or the condemned cell. There is a massive consistency about his life and words. Thus, Gerhard Leibholz in his memoir of Dietrich Bonhoeffer wrote:

> In prison and concentration camps, Bonhoeffer greatly inspired by his indomitable courage, his unselfishness and his goodness, all those who came into contact with him. He even inspired his guards with respect, some of whom became so attached to him that they smuggled out of prison his papers and poems.[4]

Yet there are those who testify to the fact that the quality of Christian spirit Bonhoeffer demonstrated in his imprisonment and death characterized his entire life. It was not his heroic death alone that attested his Christian faith. It is sometimes as punishing to live out one's faith through laborious and routine days as to go out in one glorious burst of martyrdom.

We have come the long way round from Jeremy Taylor's

tract via the empty hills around Tekoa to the recognition that the prophet's liberty in prophesying is won, like the manumission of a slave, at a price. The journalistic perception of the prophet as a free-swinging, outrageously irreverent wild man with his axe at the root of the tree must yield before Paul's firm insistence that the prophet is part of a ministry whose work is to edify the Church – to accomplish not a demolition but a restoration job. The prophet edifies the Church by helping to purify its mind, keep its conscience tender and to distil one over-arching Christian purpose from its much speaking, praying and witnessing.

As Isaiah put it, "You shall build the old waste places; you shall raise up the foundations of many generations; and you shall be called repairer of the breach, the restorer of paths to dwell in."

THREE

MINSTREL FOR THE TELEVISION AGE

It may seem frivolous or even profane to describe the august Charles Wesley as a minstrel, and even more bizarre to imply that this eighteenth-century divine and poet speaks with particular power to the TV Age. I hope to prove both points, but let's dispose of the implied slur immediately.

To designate Charles Wesley the supreme minstrel of the Methodist movement is not to surrender him to show-biz, but it is to locate him at the popular or people's end of the communications trade. Minstrels were, as the Saxons called them, "gleemen" who performed at fairs and in taverns – and that could hardly be an inappropriate name for a hymnodist who wrote "Thrice happy I am, and my heart it doth dance at the sound of His name".

In a different culture, minstrels as troubadors were men of high social standing at the centre of affairs. It was a troubador called Taillefer who led the Normans in the march on Hastings. Then again, minstrels could be fiery radicals, formenting uprisings with their protest songs on behalf of the oppressed, as in the fourteenth-century peasants' rising or in Jack Cade's rebellion a hundred years later.

And it's worth noting that the word "minstrel" in both Latin and French is derived from the same root as "minister". So it is a profession with honourable antecedents, encompassing a wide variety of roles – all of them to do with telling stories in music and verse.

I particularly associate Charles Wesley with those minstrels who were the bards of the ancient Celtic peoples, the Gauls, Britons, Welsh, Irish and Scots – although not, I hasten to add, in appearance, dress or demeanour. It is not easy to picture the fastidious Charles dressed in animal skins and plastered with woad, sitting round a camp fire strumming a lyre and making wild whooping noises. But I insist he is of that lineage in the history of communication, and so I'm not disposed to be too particular about the social details.

The Celtic minstrels were tribal dignitaries who celebrated the deeds of gods and heroes, stirred up the people for battle, and recorded tribal history in verse. They were masters of epic, satire and panegyric – in other words, they celebrated the heroic deeds of their people, poked fun at them for the good of their souls and then said good words about them as they were laid to rest alongside their ancestors.

The minstrels were the incarnate memory-banks of the Celts.[5] They survived in Ireland and Wales, two nations of compulsive gossips, story-tellers and natural talkers, long after they had disappeared elsewhere. The traditional bard appeared before the people in the guise of a popular entertainer but he had a more complex role. He was the arbiter of language, coining metaphors and phrases which reinforced the tribe's identity and marked it off from its neighbours.

On the whole, minstrels were not prophets, confronting people with uncomfortable truths, addressing the encampment from the edge of the desert. They spoke from the centre of culture, not its periphery. They were the guardians of tribal orthodoxy. Theirs was the authorized version, the distillation of the collective memory. They dragged out long-forgotten ancient wisdom, dusted it off and made it relevant.

Above all, minstrels were superb communicators, who married words to music in songs that stuck in the memory and so could be reproduced at will. They were rallying points in times of disruption and confusion, helping to hold things together by celebrating common identity and affirming truths all the people ought to agree on. Just, in fact, like Charles Wesley.

The Rhythms of Religion

From time immemorial, people have celebrated in song and dance the most profound experiences of their lives — life and death, joy and tragedy, communion and loneliness. From the ancient Israelites dancing before the Ark of the Lord to mourners in rural Ireland returning from a funeral on a farm cart to the accompaniment of a fiddler playing an Irish jig, humanity has set its deepest hopes and fears to music and entrusted them to a minstrel to preserve and express in song . . .

. . . In song, because music, poetry and dance engage the human personality at more levels than can speech. They strike deep into the psyche to express things too soul-shaking or too ambiguous to render into prose. Gustav Mahler confessed that he only began to compose music because he could never put his feelings into words. And Spinoza insisted that an emotion can never be explained by reason; only by a stronger emotion.

Music underlines all the central areas of human experience. During the freedom struggle in Africa, when colonial governments imprisoned nationalist leaders or banned them from addressing meetings, the message of freedom still spread like wildfire because the people incarnated it in popular songs. It was possible to muzzle the orator and disperse the crowd, but there was no way of stopping the people from singing. Little wonder that the Scottish patriot, Fletcher of Saltoun, wrote, "Let me make a country's songs, then who will can make its laws".

Music and religion have this in common. At their centre is rhythm – a pulsating flow which resonates with something utterly fundamental at the very heart of things. To move with this rhythm is to be fulfilled; to get cross-grained to it is to feel alienation and unease – disharmony. Is there any torture so exquisite as having to endure music we do not understand? Or any desolation so great as seeking God without success? A long time ago Confucius noted this affinity between music and religion. He wrote, "In music of the grandest style, there is the same harmony that prevails between heaven and earth" – a sense of wholeness, of things being as they were intended to be.

Therefore, in the evolution of religion, the minstrel has primacy over the theologian because until there is something to celebrate, some event or experience to mark ceremonially, there is nothing to reflect on. According to the preface of the 1933 Methodist Hymn Book, "Methodism was born in song". So are most religions. The American philosopher of religion, A. D. Nock, said that a primitive religion had to be danced and sung before it could be believed.

One eminent contemproary theologian, asked whether he could conscientiously recite the Apostles' Creed, replied, "No, but I can sing it!" Exactly. We can sing beyond our conscious beliefs because the many layers of meaning in music and poetry can accommodate that agnosticism which is inevitable when reaching out for God, who by definition is beyond the range of our senses.

The charismatic preacher or leader may bring into existence a new religious movement, but it is usually the minstrel who fixes the cardinal points of the experience in the minds of the followers. In this way faith is rendered memorable and can be carried around in the head from place to place. That is what Charles Wesley, as minstrel of the Methodist movement, did: he encapsulated teaching in a form that was unforgettable. And in this sense, he planted theological time-bombs in the mind. Hymns Methodists learned in Sunday School, whose words they didn't fully understand or had forgotten, in later life exploded with new meaning like long-buried seeds bursting through into the light.

When I was a missionary in Africa, I visited a mission station run by the White Fathers in Zambia's Northern Province. I was the first Methodist most of these French and Dutch Catholic missionaries had encountered. Politely but firmly they enquired about Methodist sacramental theology. To my shame, I confess I could not recall a single word John Wesley had written on the subject. Then there came to mind the words of Charles Wesley's communion hymn, "Victim Divine, Thy grace we claim . . . ". Honour was satisfied. They admitted to being very impressed by Methodism's high doctrine of the Eucharist.

Inspired Opportunism

Many of the exciting new twists in the Christian story over the centuries have occurred because advocates for Christianity have exploited developments in communications technology. For instance, Christianity came to birth in a world which enjoyed the *Pax Romana* – a communications environment consisting of a network of good roads, sound public order and a community of language in various combinations of Latin and Greek. The apostles were able to reach the maximum number of communities and address them with some hope of being understood.

The manuscript era which followed the age of the apostles created the literate clerk or clergyman, and made university theologians in the high Middle Ages the power behind papal and episcopal thrones. The age of print made it possible to put a Bible in anybody's hands, established the Reformation, accelerated literacy, inspired religious individualism and allowed Luther to appeal to Scripture against the Pope. Print made easier the exact and mass reproduction of complex ideas, authoritative texts and abstract definitions– all the grand tradition of theology, in fact.

Charles Wesley, too, was a great innovator. He used what was available as a medium of mass communication. And providentially to hand was the austere, classical metre used to such magisterial effect by Milton, Dryden and Pope. It was a literary form characterized by order, proportion, discipline and clarity – the ideal vehicle for hymnwriting. Had Charles Wesley been born half a century later, during the Romantic Revival when the verse was of a straggling kind in which discipline gave way to emotion and austerity to ornateness, he would have been swimming against the tide in trying to produce hymns that were memorable, simple and restrained.

Wesley was a mass communicator who reached the ordinary people with an astonishing range of themes. He wrote no fewer than six thousand hymns, and as the Methodist historian Rupert Davies comments, "In this vast corpus there is a great deal that is banal, still more that is merely repetitive, and much employment of images which now strike us as grotesque."[6]

But this is the inevitable price the popular communicator pays for blanket coverage – sheer quantity swamping quality. The fastidious poet can work and rework lines until they are polished and perfect. The minstrel is no Poet Laureate who descends from his eyrie to pen some grandiloquent lines for a great occasion and then lapses into brooding silence. He must record the totality of the life of his people, much of which is routine and unremarkable; his verse will reflect the fact.

Mass communicators, whatever their medium, deal in ephemerality. Their work is intended to be used up in the first flush of composition. It is the sheer quantity of their output which makes its impact in creating an ethos and permeating an environment. Should any of this work be of such a quality that it comes to be regarded as a classic, living on beyond one generation, then that is a bonus. But the basic aim is to motivate, not to decorate.

Yet just as television and radio have their big occasions, so too had Charles Wesley. Though he occasionally sinks to the depths, he more often rises to the heights, and having risen to them is capable of staying on them for a remarkably long time.

John Wesley was a severe critic of his brother's hymnody – he rejected an early draft of "Jesu, Lover of My Soul" as being mawkish and over-sentimental – so the verdict he renders on the poetry of the 1780 Hymn Book in its Preface will bear pondering. There is, he insists, "no doggerel, no botches, nothing put in to patch up the rhyme, no feeble expletives . . . nothing turgid or bombast or low and creeping . . . no cant expressions, no words without meaning . . . We talk common sense."

And a hymn book is, after all, an artefact of mass communication. The compilers of *Hymns Ancient and Modern* wrote, "A good hymn book is necessarily an endeavour in high democracy. The life-time of a hymn is one which congregations decide by an unconscious process." High democracy . . . the people decide. The minstrel seeks the approval not of the judges of the Oxford Poetry Prize but of the generality of believers.

This is surely one of the clearest evidences of that Reformation doctrine, the priesthood of all believers. The laity may not be able to choose the cardinal doctrines of their faith – the charismatic leaders and sacred conclaves do that – but they can decide which popular expressions of the faith will prevail. They vote not with their feet but with their voices. Their stubborn insistence on cherishing some hymns and studiously neglecting others decides the shape and content of the people's apologetic.

But it is not the quality of the words alone which give the minstrel's utterance power. The magic is in the wedding of the words to music. For as Schleiermacher said, "What the word makes clear, music makes alive". Salvation, as Charles Wesley wrote, comes as "music to the sinner's ear". It is music which fixes the words in the memory. If we are uncertain of the words of a song, we hum its melody and find the lyric coming back to us.

The earliest hymns of the Reformation were those of the Bohemian Brethren, and every attempt to suppress their hymnody by book-burning failed because the Brethren could reconstruct the contents of their hymn books from memory. Were all the sermons and writings of John Wesley to be destroyed, the main outlines of his theology could be reconstituted from memory by a devotee of the hymns of his brother. In much the same way, the sermons of the Victorian evangelist Dwight Moody are read no more, but their themes still echo in some evangelical circles through *Sacred Songs and Solos*, the revivalist hymn book published by Moody's singing companion, Sankey.

When we talk of "learning something by heart", we are speaking of more than a feat of memory; it is making truth part of our inner selves, for the heart is the traditional seat of the soul. And setting that knowledge to music is the most potent way of involving the whole person and not just the eyes or ears.

So Charles Wesley exploited the most powerful communications medium of his day to spread the Gospel. Before the advent of sound amplification, mass singing was the only effective way of achieving intelligibility in spaces too large to be filled by the unaided preaching voice. And though early Methodist congregations were modest in size compared to the mass choirs of the Moody evangelical campaigns, and later those of Billy Graham, their singing was marked by a potent combination of harmonic discipline and emotional freedom.

The American poet Walt Whitman wrote, "In all true religious fervour there is a touch of animal heat". This passion thundered through Methodist singing as great congregations roared in rapture. But it was not mindless; not heat without light. Charles Wesley offered no moronic gospel jingles, no endlessly repetitive choruses of brain-numbing banality. He was obsessed by big themes – the central drama of God's dealings with the human soul, expressed in the incarnation of Jesus and apprehended

67

through the believer's personal experience. So not just vocal cords but minds were stretched, and spiritual experience deepened.

The Age of the Electronic Story-Teller

There would seem to be a great gulf fixed between the classical poetry of the Augustan Age, Charles Wesley's chosen medium, and the soap-opera vacuity of the TV era. There are, however, two qualities of television as a medium which also characterize Charles Wesley's hymnody. The first is its role as a story-teller; the second is its power as an image maker.

Television is an electronic story-teller. All its programmes, not just drama or comedy, are cast in the form of narrative – from the weather forecast to the half-minute commercial. The shaping of programmes into story form, with a beginning, a middle and an end, is made inevitable by the time constraints and scheduling patterns by which television operates. There can be no loose ends; there must be resolution. One programme must be concluded to the viewer's satisfaction to make way for the next programme, which is likely to be about an entirely different subject.

Charles Wesley was a superb story-teller. Consider that hymn known as "Wrestling Jacob" – "Come, O Thou traveller unknown" – based on Jacob's encounter with God at the ford of the River Jabbok. The great Isaac Watts declared that this one hymn was worth all the verses he had written. Or note the narrative drive compressed into just three words in one line from Wesley's great Easter hymn, "Christ the Lord is risen today" – "Ours the **cross**, the **grave**, the **skies**." That is not just a spiritual history of the believer but a summary of the modes of being of the Christian Church: cross, martyrdom; grave, passivity; skies, renewal.

Story-telling has been central to Christianity from the beginning, because the Gospel is not a body of teaching nor a Platonic dialogue but an account of something *done*. It is cast in the classic form of drama – happening, development, crisis and resolution.

Theology as story has two central themes. There is the miraculous turn of grace expressed through the great polarities of life – decay and renewal, sudden ends and new beginnings, death and resurrection, peril and safety. The other great theme of religious story is that of journeying, in space, time and condition. The search for a destination, the attempt to find the way home, the struggle towards an Answer sent Muslims journeying to Mecca, pilgrims to Canterbury, Catholics to Rome, the Greeks to Delphi and druids to Stonehenge. The journey is inspired by crisis, undertaken in faith, beset by danger and culminates in a great firework display of welcome at the destination.

The parable of the Prodigal Son illustrates to perfection both the theme of the miraculous turn of grace – "This my son was *dead* and is *alive*, was *lost* and is *found*" – and the theme of journeying. Sick of Home, Homesick, Home was the homiletical structure once used by the great twentieth-century Methodist preacher, Dr W. E. Sangster, to expound the parable.

The Christian journey at whose end the weary believer is amazed by a miraculous turn of grace is a constant preoccupation of Charles Wesley – "Captain of Israel's host, and Guide of all who seek the land above"; "Come all who'er have set your faces Zion-ward"; "Leader of faithful souls, and Guide of all that travel to the sky"; "A stranger in the world below, I calmly sojourn here"; "Jesu, my Truth, my Way"; "Love divine, all loves excelling, Joy of heaven to earth come down" – and so on and on.

All true religious narratives are, in the phrase of the American New Testament scholar, Sallie TeSelle, "stories of coming to belief". Examining the beliefs themselves is an intellectual exercise, the work of technical theologians. But ordinary believers can identify with the titanic struggle of a human being to win through the fog to the light on the horizon's rim. And non-believers, too. For they may find they face the choice of accepting static meaninglessness or risking the adventure of the perilous journey of faith.

The other property of television which has resonances with Charles Wesley's verse is its power as an image maker. The television age is the first since the Renaissance in which the word has been displaced by the image as the chief means by which popular culture is transmitted. This is not to say that words are unimportant, but increasingly they serve the image rather than the idea in the thought-world of ordinary people.

Television takes us back beyond the ages of literacy to a more primitive state, for as Freud said, the image preceded the idea in the development of human consciousness. It was a world full of images of divine power and mystery; a more religious world than ours because, as George Caird has written, "Belief in God depends to a small extent on rational argument, and to a larger extent on our ability to frame images to capture, commemorate and convey our experience of transcendence."[7]

Charles Wesley was a master of the vivid, compressed image which burned itself into the mind and heart and became unforgettable through constant rehearsal in worship. Take his account of the Incarnation – phrases such as "Our God, contracted to a span", "Emptied himself of all but love", "Veiled in flesh the Godhead see", "Being's source begins to be", "Dwelling in an earthly clod, whom Heaven cannot contain" and "Will Thy majesty stoop down to so mean a house as this?" – such sumptuous imagery encapsulates in a single snapshot a whole theological argument.

His vignettes are unforgettable – "the scars his dear disfigured body bears", "the pointless darts of death", "changed from glory into glory"; "Lift poor dying worms to heaven", "Christ, whose glory fills the skies", "Vain the stone, the watch, the seal", "Soften, melt and pierce and break an adamantine heart", "Soar we now where Christ hath led", and that heart-stopping phrase, stark and incontestable, in the commemoration hymn about the host passing over the flood of death – "And some are crossing now".

The image affirms where the idea often divides. Take that glorious phrase, "Our God, contracted to a span" – radicals and evangelicals, catholics and liberals sing it with great gusto at church assemblies. And yet analyse each word forensically and you'll have the theological schools in uproar. There is the stuff of endless argument in the words, yet the image affirms an incontestable truth.

Thanks to their supreme minstrel, the Methodist people have never been deprived of luminous images in which to enshrine their deepest experiences. Charles Wesley left no central doctrines unexplored, no profound spiritual depths uncharted. And like all true minstrels, he recorded not just what the people believed, but what they could believe, what was on offer through the munificent grace of God.

Scanning the theological range and depth of Wesley's

hymnody, it would be a confident believer who could, hand on heart, declare, "Yes, I believe all that!" But the minstrel took the often pedestrian beliefs of the moment and idealized, romanticized and intensified them. So too, at a time when it was said the bishops were agnostic about everything except the quality of wines in their cellar, Charles Wesley stood for the conviction that if one is to have a faith at all, let it be a full-blooded one. For Christianity and water will neither get anyone drunk with Spirit or even set the religious taste buds a-tingling.

Charles Wesley's rich store of imagery was owed not just to a fertile imagination and a fluent pen; it was massively scriptural. There are biblical echoes in every hymn, and occasionally he manages to weave both Old and New Testament themes into a single line. These biblical images, symbols and stories are what Sallie TeSelle calls "root metaphors", because it is not possible to break them down further or go behind them. They are as close to divine mystery as language can get. They are not intended to be analysed into their constituent parts; they offer insight and disclosure by pointing beyond themselves to the transcendent.

In that much lampooned television programme, *Songs of Praise*, Christian congregations gather in a local church to sing well-known hymns chosen by members of the community who are interviewed about their choice. Millions of people watch it who would never dream of attending church on Sunday. Is it just an orgy of nostalgia, or is the electronic bard jogging some nerve and stirring up society's collective memory? The great festival hymns of Charles Wesley are one way in which rich biblical imagery still permeates the consciousness of a generation that doesn't know its Bible.

Many people obviously feel the need for some place in modern society where traditional values are affirmed, corporate identity is reinforced and the robustness of folk religion celebrated. The hymns in *Songs of Praise* recall key events in national and personal life, and the physical setting, a church, has all kinds of resonances for a people whose history and tradition are firmly rooted in the Christian faith.

And the interviews in the programme with Christians who are wrestling with appalling problems and battling against great handicaps are powerful and disturbing pieces of testimony. It is significant that when they cast around for a way of summarizing their crisis and describing how faith has helped them to survive it, they appeal to some well-loved hymn. And it is Charles Wesley who often supplies the images that say it all.

Even a maturely secular society finds it hard to evolve alternative imagery to that of the Bible because new myths are not easily invented. The myths that sustain a people arise from their common history, tradition and experience. And the biblical myth is significant because it evokes central themes of the human story on which Western society has based its life for a thousand years – creation, fall, trial and restoration; primitive bliss, exile from paradise, suffering, death and rebirth; the life and death struggle of the hero; disruption, catastrophe, vindication and the return of order.

It is taken for granted that contemporary society is secular, but the truth is more complex. Its traditions were formed in a Christian world and much public symbolism reflects the fact, from prayers each day before sittings of Parliament to the singing of "Abide with me" at Cup Finals. Much public disclosure about morals is conducted in a Christian vocabulary, and many popular sayings, expressions of folk wisdom and turns of speech are derived from the Bible, the Book of Common Prayer, hymnody and a literary heritage decisively influenced by Christianity.

Britain's spiritual ethos is an amalgam of nostalgia, folk religion, monarchist sentiment (which has religious overtones) and love of tradition, shot through with the convictions of various religious orthodoxies. And the ghost of the biblical God still haunts the collective memory of the people, even though only a minority make conscious acknowledgement of his existence.

Thus, my contention would be that Charles Wesley's hymnody helps to jog the nerve of our society about the biblical myth which lies deep in its heart, beneath more recent myths to do with secular progress and economic self-sufficiency. Television, for all its faults, is putting story-telling back at the heart of popular culture. And because it conveys all its key messages in images, it is helping to restore the visual imagination.

It is often charged that television has undermined organized religion by wooing people away from church attendance, and has let loose across the ether a flood of pagan detritus. Paradoxically the medium may actually be stimulating human faculties that are hospitable to faith. For if television is in the business of telling gripping stories in striking images, then Charles Wesley, with his mastery of both, may well be the minstrel for the TV Age – the religious communicator who feeds a newly revivified visual imagination with evocative pictures of what salvation could mean.

FOUR

CELLULOID
SAVIOURS

Amos Wilder, in his book *Jesus' Parables and the War of Myths*, writes: "That story-telling has such a central place in the very beginning of the Gospel means more than may at first appear. It was not merely to hold the attention of his hearers that [Jesus] told stories or took good illustrations out of his file. There was something in the nature of the case that evoked this rhetoric, something in the nature of the Gospel."

This "something in the nature of the case" could only be that the Gospel embodies not just *a* story but *the* story – the primary plot which underlies the countless narrative lines expressed in the whole corpus of literature and drama. *The* plot takes us way back beyond deep down under our own civilization to the dawn of story-telling itself; to that first occasion on which one human being said to another, as both huddled together round a fire to keep out the encroaching dark, "Once upon a time . . .".

I think this is a rejoinder to those who challenge the truth of Christianity on the grounds that it is not the record of a unique series of events; other religions offer accounts of virgins giving birth, gods becoming men, dying and rising again. This doesn't prove that Christianity is just a Jewish facsimile of Greek mythology or Hindu religion, but shows that it is a truly incarnate faith, securely anchored in the real world of religious truth. There must be some overlap in religious experience between different cultures, otherwise the human race is a fiction – each society and era an air-tight compartment to which there is no access from the outside.

The religious experiences of an ancient Egyptian, a twelfth-century Aztec, a Sioux Indian and a modern Western Christian must have the same strand of truth in them, however differently their myths describe it. How broad a strand is a different matter. I am not suggesting for one moment that all religions have roughly the same proportion of truth and error in them; merely insisting that the truth is given by God, and what human beings do with that truth is there for all to see in the myths they cherish, the deities they worship and the laws they obey.

That primordial truth haunts The Story – life as a journey towards some destination with pitfalls, terrors and joys along the way, and somewhere on the road a crisis travellers cannot resolve for themselves; they need the intervention of a hero or a saviour who against the odds embodies a miraculous turn of grace.

The Story persists regardless of the fortunes of organized religion. One way or another, the story of the human predicament resolved by the intervention of a superhuman Hero will get itself told, not just solemnly through serious literature but as a theme in popular culture. And since the cinema and television have become the most powerful story-tellers of our time, we would expect to see it portrayed on the large or small screen. So let's take a look at some of the celluloid saviours of our time.[8]

Saviours on Horseback

The cowboy Western is as stylized as a poem and it moves to its predictable end with the inevitability of a morality play. Regular cinema and TV viewers know the end from the beginning because they have been weaned on the half-a-dozen or so variations of the standard plot. Before a word has been spoken, they can distinguish the hero from the villain by the cut of his dress, the way he treats his horse or even the style of his saloon-bar slouch.

The world of the Western is one of bloody innocence in which all men are equal, and the symbol of their equality is the six-gun. The hundred-pound weakling, if he's quick on the draw, is more than a match for the twenty-stone bully. The gun is the basis of civilization and the guarantor of instant justice. The ethic that controls its use couldn't be simpler – you don't draw first and you never ever shoot a woman. Women occasionally do get shot, but that's because of their silly habit of throwing themselves protectively in front of their lover.

All human problems are solved by dispatching them to the Boot Hill cemetery. No need for psychology, theories of communication, the sheer sweat of human relations. Flying bullets resolve all. And in this crazy code of honour, there is only one mortal sin – cowardice, the refusal to draw. It is the willingness to lay one's life on the line for a handful of dust that defines true manliness.

There are of course type-cast weaklings in the Western-men who will not carry a gun – the preacher, for instance, with beard, Bible and numerous progeny; the doctor, who is often a reformed gunman; and the teacher, who fights a losing battle to convince gun-hungry kids that there is another world beyond the foresight of a Winchester rifle.

Things rule supreme in the Western; it is a world where

materialism has been carried to its ultimate conclusion. It is rare that an idea, a concept or an abstract value sets the guns thundering. A gold strike, a battle for land or cattle starts the action, and pure greed primes the pumps. And because a happy ending for our side is mandatory, as in the Greek tragedy, final resolution is achieved through cataclysm, the gun-fight at the O.K. Corral.

Laramie, Fort Apache, Abilene or Sante Fe are depicted as communities of decent if callow citizens hiding behind locked doors whilst villains rampage throughout the town. The local law is corrupt or weak, ordinary people are at the mercy of evildoers. Anarchy and chaos loom. The moral stereotypes are simple and absolute.

Then into town rides a saviour bearing redemption and retribution in his gun holsters. He is an outsider, a man from nowhere. As the story wears on, he reveals only sufficient of his history to explain his actions. Alan Ladd's *Shane* and Clint Eastwood's *Man with No Name* are god-men who come down from the Western Valhalla and are suddenly incarnate in a situation of extreme conflict. They resolve matters and then ride off into the sunset – a secular Ascension. Indeed, when the hero of *The Man with No Name* prepares himself for the dénouement, he puts on a clerical collar. There are subtler ways of indicating that divine retribution is at hand.

The hero's motivation varies but it is located somewhere along a narrow spectrum of moral attitudes. He may have a sense of chivalry that places him in the tradition of medieval knights and Japanese samurai – "a man's gotta do what a man's gotta do!" He may be out to right old wrongs – "Why? I knew someone like you once, and nobody helped her", explains Clint Eastwood in *A Fistful of Dollars*. Or it may just be destiny: as the gunfighter

Nobody puts it in *My Name is Nobody*, "A hero can't run away from his destiny. Sometimes you run smack into your destiny on the very same road you take away from it."

The hero is more than an angel of vengeance; he brings into being a new moral order. Down come the barricades, citizens venture out about their business again, children laugh and play in the streets, the church bell rings out, the town drunk sobers up in the horse trough, and the saloon girls catch the next stage to Dodge City. New Jerusalem bears an uncanny resemblance to the American Dream.

It is not just the moral sentiments of the Western that echo religious aphorisms, the bit players in the drama often ape characters who would fit neatly into the gospels. Whilst the respectable citizens spurn the hero, it is the outcasts who befriend and support him. The saloon girl with the heart of gold and the town drunk stand by him when everyone else flees. And like the penitent thief on the cross, there is always one villain who testifies wrily in his dying breath to the hero's moral superiority.

Sometimes the hero survives and is left standing with smoking guns in a desolation of corpses. Sometimes he dies in a hail of bullets with a suitably ennobling sentiment on his lips. And yet he does not die but lives on in the hearts and minds of the grateful living – to inspire the young and give those of least social account a sense of their own self-worth. "He didn't laugh at me", says the town simpleton wonderingly.

The temptation to draw biblical parallels is almost irresistible, for the Western genre seems to parody the Gospel, though probably quite unconsciously. It is that Story, which lives deep down in the psyche of the human race, haunts its dreams and teases its imagination, surfacing in the least likely places – such as a saloon bar in the old West.

Saviours with Scalpels

But what about those stories whose heroes are not concerned with the judicial taking of life but with the attempt to save it – the medical epics of the cinema and television? In the beginning was the Baroque Age of medical science in films, where "doctor" was a catch-all term for a scientist able to turn his hand to anything from inventing death rays to giving an Egyptian mummy a heart transplant. Because in the real world doctors deal in life or death, so from the very outset in films they were invested with god-like powers, capable of creating Frankenstein's monster or the Invisible Man at will.

The standard scenario was of a brilliant but demented surgeon at work in an underground dungeon, surrounded by foaming test-tubes, doing unspeakable things to some village dolt who happened to fall into his hands. The resulting monster proves to have a genetic structure unknown to *decent* medical science – a noble discipline represented by the mad-scientist's anti-type, a country GP, equipped with Gladstone bag, pony and trap and Lionel Barrymore's eyebrows.

So in the beginning doctors were portrayed on films as superhuman, either devils or saints. They were living metaphors of Good and Evil – burning themselves out in slum surgeries or mission hospitals trying to save life, or misusing their skills to destroy the world or change the whole direction of evolution. When the Baroque Age gave way to the Romantic Era, doctors lost none of their divinity. They just got more cuddly.

Across the cinema screen glided a succession of handsome, young healers, glowing with zeal and innocence – of which they were smartly disabused by their crusty old mentors who brilliantly concealed hearts of pure gold beneath their mildewed frock coats. Kildare had his Dr Gillespie; Finlay, his Dr Cameron. It was a trade-off: though the young doctor had attended a modern medical school, the old doctor had lived. In each episode the grey-beard took on board a new idea, whilst the callow youth learned an old lesson about human nature.

These god-like creatures were loved – by patients, hope-lessly; by nurses, secretly; by women colleagues, against their better judgement; even by their wives. And for histri-onics, no setting could compare with an operating theatre. For nowhere else could be crammed into a confined space such a witch's brew of life and death drama, intense love interest, technological mystification, morbid curiosity and even a touch of the sinister – those masked and green-gowned figures hunched over a member of the public.

Young Doctor Kildare was the embodiment of a scien-tific age's saviour figure – clean-cut, idealistic, dedicated and above all a miracle-worker. So the drama unfolds – the child's headache becomes a fever, then a life-threaten-ing illness. The family doctor is baffled; the hospital staff have never seen anything like it. Enter the saviour. Dr Kildare frowns, then recalls an obscure article in a medical journal. "Will she live, Dr Kildare?" is the question torn from the mother's anguished heart, and five hundred people in the cinema stalls twist their handkerchiefs and wait, joining with the patient in searching anxiously those gorgeous brown eyes for an answer. He smiles com-passionately, "There's this new wonder drug . . .".

Dr Kildare is totally incarnate in the crisis. His is a magnificent obsession; he lives only to heal. Apart from the most innocent of emotional attachments, he has no private life. He never visits his parents, apparently takes no time off, doesn't play golf and it is unthinkable that he should get drunk. He is pure, beautiful and radiates health. His grateful patients draw life from him. It is as though in healing their bodies he mends their lives and they become whole and happy. An appropriate saviour indeed for an age with a pathetic faith in the power of science to work miracles and stave off disease, death and disaster.

Saviour Clowns

Make a wrenching change of gear to acknowledge a celluloid saviour whose secret weapon is neither a six-gun nor a scalpel but laughter. The healing and renewing gift comes equipped with bowler hat, knobbly cane and big feet – the cinema clown; and pre-eminently Charlie Chaplin.

The clown pits innocent goodness against brutality and evil, whether embodied in the bullying policeman and beetle-browed villain or in the dehumanizing complexities of life, such as the soulless city and the factory production line. And he is bound to lose. He ends up bruised and dishevelled in the gutter, but dusts himself off, shrugs his shoulders and limps away, whistling. He refuses to conform to the limits of what sensible people call the possible. He *will* insist on riding a bicycle whose wheels are out of kilter or trying to walk along a slack tightrope – with inevitable results. He just insists on living out his dreams, and is prepared to pay the price for the privilege.

Chaplin as clown uses the strategy of laughter as a protest against the vicious and dehumanizing forces of life. Take three of his famous films, each of which had a great social evil as its target – *City Lights* attacked the soullessness of modern urban life; *Modern Times* challenged the mindlessness of endlessly repetitive labour; and *The Great Dictator* exposed the heartlessness of totalitarianism. The clown is an affectionate social critic who would echo Voltaire's prayer, "O Lord, make my enemies ridiculous!" Without rancour or hatred, he makes fun of his enemies, and soon everyone is laughing at them.

This is the strategy which was used by inmates of Nazi concentration camps to assert their essential humanity in conditions of ultimate depravity. They would make open fun of their captors, and in so doing show that ultimate power is not exercised by those with life or death control over others but by those who can laugh at them.

And the Chaplinesque clown is a vulnerable lover. There is a ritual ending to virtually every one of Charlie Chaplin's films, where the Sweet Young Thing who has befriended him and shared his misadventures rushes towards him with her arms outspread. Charlie, amazed and delighted, steps forward, only to find it's the good looking bloke standing next to him whom the girl embraces. Charlie never gets the girl. But his unwillingness to learn is only exceeded by his incurable expectancy. When the next film opens, there he goes again, splay-footed, after another hopeless love.

It is the clown's fate to be a vulnerable lover. Because his heart is bursting with loving-kindness towards his fellow men and women, there is no room in his head for the thought that anyone might bear him ill-will in return. Not once, but a dozen times in each film, Charlies goes up to a bully with a smile on his face – and is punched on the nose for his pains. But he keeps on trying. For his working philosophy is that the universe is benign, people are basically good and that love will take the chill off the coldest heart. And he's got the bruises to prove it. It is deadly innocence; the beguiling power of hopefulness.

The clown is a free spirit who saves people from the machine-like conformity and drudgery by daring them to tackle life his way. Harvey Cox is one modern theologian who had described Christ as a clown; he finds elements in the biblical portrait of Jesus which have resonances with clown-like behaviour. He writes, "Only by learning to laugh at the hopelessness around us can we touch the hem of hope. Christ the clown signifies our playful appreciation of the past and our comic refusal to accept the spectre of inevitability in the future. He is the incarnation of festivity and fantasy."[9]

Saviour – Special Agent

Another celluloid saviour who is decidedly not given to taking a thump on the nose without retaliation and who, unlike Chaplin, *always* gets the girl, is James Bond – 007, who transforms vices into virtues by the sheer verve with which he pursues them.

Bond is a supreme exponent of the art of pain, both inflicting and suffering it – always portrayed with scientific exactitude, spasm by spasm, scream after scream. It is salvation by suffering. Bond wins because he can absorb more punishment than his adversaries and then strike the final blow. And it is all rendered morally acceptable because Bond is the good guy, killing for the sake of democracy and because his masters tell him to.

Then there is the egregious snobbery. Bond would die rather than smoke a cheap cigarette, drive a mass-produced car, make love to a plain woman or wear suits off the peg. Everything, from his custom-made shoes to his vintage souped-up Bentley, is an essential element in a life style into which nothing ordinary or pedestrian is allowed to intrude. The materialism of it all is so pure that it refines itself into a form of spirituality.

Bond's enemies are automata fuelled by greed. They also tend to be non-white, but that's a different story. Greed as such is not an offence in Bond's world. The rich are entitled to inherit the earth: only when one of them wants the whole lot is his doom sealed. Bond is the Nemesis of the ultra greedy on behalf of the unashamedly affluent.

There are no moral complexities or ethical dilemmas in Bond's universe. There is our side and theirs, grateful allies and dead enemies. Bond exists in a moral vacuum; he neither weighs the human consequences of his actions beforehand nor engages in retrospection after the event. He just reloads his Werner automatic pistol, packs his custom-made luggage and heads off for the next assignment.

The nearest Bond ever gets to conventional morality – apart from a kind of chivalry which lays claim to a lady's virtue as the price for saving her life – is patriotism. He kills in the national interest in an act of blind, unquestioning obedience. He does not challenge the judgement of his anonymous master, possibly because a conscience cannot be purchased over the counter at Harrods. He is post-moral man who kills without remorse, loves without commitment and spends life without replenishing it. He is Super-Sinner who holds a magnetic attraction for a world which finds the saint either an enigma or a bore.

Bond is the ultimate male chauvinist. He is incapable of or uninterested in establishing any relationship with a woman except for the purposes of sex; even the playful rapport with his boss's secretary, Miss Moneypenny, hints at unrequited love on her part and a tantalizing promise on his. It is interesting that when he fails to seduce Tilly Masterson in *Goldfinger*, Bond diagnoses the problem as her hormones getting mixed up — "a direct consequence of giving the vote to women".

007 is a celluloid saviour who saves humanity, or at least, our bit of it, by a combination of animal courage, savage single-mindedness and technical virtuosity. He can turn a cigarette lighter into a death ray, escape from a volcano's burning crater on a rocket-propelled back-pack, and open a locked safe by turning the dial of his wrist watch.

He is in the strict sense of the term the Anti-Christ of the big screen. Take his values and his qualities and then match them against their mirror image. The nearest historical embodiment of everything James Bond does *not* stand for is Jesus of Nazareth. Believers concerned to present the claims of Christ to our generation need to conjure with the nature of the opposition — the Hollow Man with the golden armour who haunts the dreams of the younger generation and fills them with hopeless envy.

Saviour Superman

If James Bond is the antithesis of all Jesus was and stood for, Superman is a secular parody of him. He is the lonely weakling, despised by his fellows, who has a secret alter ego who commands unearthly power because he has come down to earth, not from Heaven but from the planet Krypton. Having been found as a baby in the crater of a meteorite, he is adopted by a Mid-West couple, yet all through his childhood hears an inner voice assuring him that his real Father above the skies has not deserted him but is entrusting him with a special mission. Significantly, his crusade against evil only begins when he is thirty years old, on the death of his stepfather.

In the persona of Clark Kent a timid journalist, Superman lives a double life, savouring the blindness of his workmates who scornfully contrast his meekness with the amazing exploits of the winged avenger who hurtles through the air on missions of rescue and vengeance. His girlfriend, Lois Lane, also aches for Clark Kent to be more like Superman, by whom she has been swept off her feet. She doesn't recognize her fuddy-duddy boy friend in the caped crusader, because he has taken his glasses off and is wearing pantomime gear.

So Clark Kent goes about his pedestrian job until the forces of evil threaten to destroy the world. Then he recalls his heavenly Father's commission and goes forth to holy war, in an epic battle banishing them. As the immortal opening announcement on radio and television shows put it, "Faster than a speeding bullet! More powerful than a locomotive! Able to leap tall buildings in a single bound! Look! Up in the sky! It's a bird! It's a plane! It's Superman! Strange visitor from another planet, who came to earth with powers and abilities far beyond those of mortal men . . . he fights a never ending battle for truth, justice and the American way."

The parallels with Jesus of Nazareth are so excruciatingly obvious they probably are genuinely unconscious. It is unlikely that even in Hollywood, film makers could be so crass. Superman is probably yet another example of the gospel story permeating a whole culture and haunting the imagination of writers and film makers who believe themselves to be secular sophisticates.[10]

The Saviour on the Screen
What, finally, of *the* celluloid Saviour, portrayals of Jesus
in films and on television? If throughout Christian history
the theologians have had great difficulty in finding some
way of describing Jesus that took full account both of his
divinity and his humanity, the film makers could hardly be
blamed for making heavy weather of the same conundrum.
They could cope with the golden God-like being or the
wild-eyed human prophet, but not at the same time.

In the beginning, film makers approached with excessive
reverence their task of translating onto film the gospel
story. The actor who played Jesus was not named; his face
was never fully seen. Furthermore he had to be of blame-
less moral reputation, totally immune from any of the
usual Hollywood scandals, and commanded to give no
press interviewes. He must not be seen in real life as
an ordinary human being with tastes and opinions, who
sweated in front of reporters or who might make grammatical slips. Was it conceivable that the Son of God might
split infinitives?

The early Jesus epics relied on the classic paintings of
the Renaissance for their costumes and set piece scenes.
Cecil B. De Mille told his director of photography to study
great works of art to formulate a lighting style. And it is
said that the resulting epic, *The King of Kings*, recreated
nearly three hundred canvases, with the crucifixion scene
being based on Rubens and Doré. In one picture Christ
might be seen through the eyes of da Vinci; in another,
Titian supplied the inspiration; for a third, Tintoretto.

Cecil B. De Mille as a great film impresario recognized
the epic possibilities of the story of Jesus – and as a shrewd
businessman saw the dangers of outraging a generally
pious public opinion in the first decades of the twentieth

century. "What other film has had two thousand years' advance publicity?", he is reputed to have said of *The King of Kings*. He was quite schizoid. As a reverent artist he sculpted the main structure of the film around great works of art, whilst the showman in him produced *jeux d'esprit* in minor scenes such as a wild and lavish party in the luxurious home of Mary Magdalene. And he managed to marry them into one convincing narrative by the sheer power of a personal vision.

But so far as De Mille and the film makers of his generation were concerned, Jesus was essentially a divine being, speaking the language of the Authorized Version and slumming it on earth for a little while before ascending to heaven in a final thundering scene, which was a marvel of lighting, special effects and glorious music.

Pier Paolo Pasolini's *The Gospel According to St Matthew*, made in 1964, broke with the old De Mille tradition, and had the additional frisson of potential scandal because Pasolini was a self-confessed Marxist. He thus brought to bear a certain judicious scepticism on St Matthew's narrative which stopped well short of irreverence. Pasolini abandoned lavish Hollywood studio sets for Italy's bleaker landscapes, and used unknown actors to play the main parts.

The key characteristic of Pasolini's Jesus is spiritual ambiguity. He is not conventionally divine as De Mille's portrayal was, nor is he unequivocally human either. He seems confused about his own identity, no doubt reflecting Pasolini's inability to make up his mind what manner of man confronts him from the pages of St Matthew's Gospel. There is an honesty in Pasolini's confusion which truly reflects the spirit of our time – a society puzzled about who and what Jesus was.

Dennis Potter had made up his mind what manner of being Jesus was when he wrote the television play *Son of Man* in 1969. His Jesus is a wild desert prophet, a barrel-chested proletarian preaching a raucous gospel of love in which *eros* rather than *agape* seemed to be the dominant element. From the golden glow of the Hollywood set to the bleak sands of Galilee, Jesus had finally been cut down to mansize. And as a warm human being he is much more accessible than De Mille's pre-Raphaelite spectre. But all that is left of his divinity is a certain facility for miracle-mongering.

Lew Grade's *Jesus of Nazareth* was made in 1977 for ATV. Grade drafted in the very best of all the skills in the film-making business – Franco Zeffirelli as director, and a script written by Anthony Burgess. Even the small cameo parts were played by stars – Ralph Richardson as Simeon, Michael York as John the Baptist, Anne Bancroft as the Magdalene. So anxious was Grade not to offend Christian susceptibilities by lapses of taste that the production had everything strong, rugged or challenging leached out of it. It was a monument to good taste, and little else.

Robert Powell played a Jesus so laid back and restrained that he came across more as a preparatory school prefect than as an apocalytpic prophet. On the scale of interpretation whose two extremes are Jesus as God and as Man, Zeffirelli's needle points dead centre to a kind of personal nullity. Nothing supernatural is to be seen; even the Annunciating Angel is a beam of light.

Jesus of Nazareth was honest, decent entertainment, and possibly quite enlightening to a generation that knows not its New Testament. But its standpoint was one of utter impartiality; it was a work not of faith nor of doubt but of spiritual neutrality. Jesus was celluloid all right, but not a celluloid saviour.

It would be ungracious to carp overmuch at Lew Grade's film, for the makers of Jesus epics, however gifted they may be, cannot come to terms with the point made by the Anglican theologian and preacher, Austin Farrer, who said that Jesus did not think human thoughts divinely but divine thoughts humanly. Because the Gospel is not a drama script, Jesus' speeches are polished literary passages. People in real life just don't talk like that. Therefore to put wodges of Gospel speech into Jesus' mouth may safeguard his divinity, since this is the only evidence we have of God speaking in earthly language — but the price is to lose any real sense of his humanity. On the other hand, to move freely away from Gospel sayings into contemporary dialogue, however inspired, results in a Jesus who, in Austin Farrer's image, can only speak human thoughts divinely.

Nevertheless, it is clear that whatever the truth about the strength or weakness of the Christian faith in the twentieth century, The Story still haunts humanity. Therefore, even in the television age, Christian preaching is not proclamation in a vacuum. There are ghostly figures flitting through the half-light of our culture capable of being given solid reality by the life-renewing power of the Gospel.

FIVE

THE THEOLOGY OF THE NINE O'CLOCK NEWS

The most widely watched of all television programmes is the News, and the charge most commonly levelled at television news bulletins is that they are endless catalogues of death, destruction and disaster. It's as though television journalists stand the old saying "No news is good news" on its head and operate on the assumption that no good news is news. What motivates television journalists, and what theological reflections are prompted by the news bulletins they construct?

Normality and the News
How do they decide in the first place what news is? The base line from which the whole process begins is that of a normal, happy, well-adjusted society – in theological terms, God's good creation, within which much human existence is routine and unremarkable. News is anything fresh and interesting which disturbs this state of affairs (the bad news) or re-inforces it in striking ways (the good news).

The reiteration of normality, the assertion that all is well in God's creation, is not news. That is a basic assumption we take for granted. If it were announced on the six o'clock news that the world is more or less round, this might seem a tedious statement of the obvious. If, however, a person of some consequence, a distinguished scientist and Fellow of the Royal Society not currently in a strait-jacket, were to declare that he had indisputable evidence that the world was flat, that would be news.

Hence, normality is not news, except in an abnormal context. The statement, "There were no shootings, bombings, muggings or incidents of arson in Milton Keynes yesterday", though reassuring to the citizens of that town, holds little interest for the generality of viewers throughout the rest of the country. But substitute "Beirut" for "Milton Keynes" and you have news.

Normality is usually inferred from silence rather than marked by an item in a news bulletin. Some people are old enough to remember the awful ritual of First World War casualty lists in national newspapers. The non-inclusion of a name was a cause for celebration. It was reassurance by silence.

To start from the assumption of a good creation makes a preponderance of so-called bad news inevitable. The bad news, however scarifying, testifies ironically to the goodness and rationality that are inherent in the countless events which go unremarked. Once good news begins to dominate the bulletins, then what is going unnoticed is the normality of a sad, bad world.

Of course, it is open to the sceptic to stand this argument on its head and take as the base-line an irrational, evil world. But here we are wrestling with a fundamental moral choice that antecedes any discussion about television news. We have to make a choice. Is evil a powerful intrusion in a good world, or goodness a heroic assertion of nobility against the odds in an evil world? We would be wise to make our minds up about that because, as someone has said, he who sits on the fence in the modern world tends to get electrocuted.

Within the limits of time and cost, the television journalist is preoccupied with a two-pronged question about me as the viewer. What has happened recently which could, however indirectly, affect my life and also intrigue me?

The important and the interesting are by no means the same. The passing of some Common Market regulation about Brussels sprout quotas may affect my life but certainly doesn't interest me to the point where I want a news bulletin to go on at length about it. On the other hand, the antics of a duck riding a skateboard may occupy my mind agreeably for a few moments without changing my life.

Built-in Bias

At this point we come up against two built-in biases, one in the television medium and the other in human nature. What sort of news both affects and intrigues me? Evil seems to have a decided advantage over good on both counts. The things that could do me and my little world harm are usually, though not always, more immediate, graphic and attention-grabbing than the things that might do me good. The effects of goodness are often subtle, longer-term and occur beyond the camera's range – in the human heart, for instance.

The teen-age thug beating the old lady to death makes a gripping story which may also be unhealthily titillating. The saga of that youth's ultimate moral rehabilitation, should it happen, is likely to be long-drawn-out and outwardly uneventful, even boring. It's an important and cheering thing to happen, but is a process rather than an

94

event: it's the difference between filming a tree growing –
imperceptible action – and filming a tornado tearing that
tree out of the ground – dramatic spectacle.

There are two properties of television as a medium
which bear directly on this issue; the first is its crudity,
the second, its vitality. Take the structural crudity of television. The combination of a small screen and a 625-line
grid favours the obvious and larger than life: images that
are clamant over those that are subtle; emphatic emotions
rather than gentle ones. The hatreds and turmoils of
human character in a flawed world are highly visible; the
camera cannot miss them. Wholesome qualities such as
love, kindness and goodness do not shout for attention.
Much of their healing work is done in secret. And television cannot cope with secrets; indeed, by definition,
broadcasting is in the business of abolishing secrets.

Or take the pagan vitality of television. It seems to
generate a life and direction of its own, almost indepen-
dent of human agency. There is an inherent excitement
about the medium that heats the blood of all programme
makers. Hence, they are tempted to accept the medium's
bare existence as self-justifying – to assume that provided
the technical questions are resolved, the value questions
will take care of themselves.

Live moving pictures have the power to sever the nerve
between sensation and meaning, event and context,
emotional spasm and deep sentiment, fact and truth.
Because of the immediacy and mobility of modern news
gathering, television news editors are confronted in every
shift with dozens of tricky judgements in this area which
must be made there and then. In my experience, they
usually make them with a sure-footedness and sensitivity
for which they are rarely given credit, because the public

does not see those horrendous pictures that never actually reach the screen.

The medium's built-in bias towards gloom and doom has to be wrestled with so that its visual enticements do not become self-justifying. But human nature also has its built-in bias which exacerbates the problem. Many people find something morbidly fascinating about violence in all its forms. It has an unhealthy hold on the public imagination. People want to know, even though they recoil in horror from what they see. They demand explicitness.

Good News about the Bad News

So there is something of the ghoul in most of us, but what about the bad newes that cannot be blamed on human beings? The human will, even at its most corrupt, cannot be held accountable for those natural disasters and calamities which take up more and more bulletin time as the techniques of news gathering become swifter and more versatile. Earthquakes, floods, drought, volcanic eruptions and fires – all those catastrophes quaintly described in the old insurance policies as Acts of God – have an added dimension of sheer irrationality which makes many viewers uneasy.

That old question of natural theology – what evidence is there of God at work in his world? – is given a new urgency by what the ordinary viewers can see on their television screens. Simply by reporting disasters and confronting viewers with them in their own sitting rooms as they happen, television news is sharpening the key questions of Christian apologetic.

The cliché has it that the world sets the agenda for any intellectual encounter between the Christian faith and the natural order. Never has the state of the world been so nakedly exposed for all to see, sketching out in flame and smoke the urgent question for the Christian theologian, teacher and preacher, "Well, what have you got to say about that?"

I doubt whether the faith of serious believers is totally undermined by shocking pictures of natural disasters. They have usually passed beyond any belief in a crudely interventionist God who punishes a recalcitrant world by thunderbolt and lightning flash. But the problem of convincing the generality of the public that God's love is at work in history is made more acute.

The Christian contends that evil in history is at all times fearsome but never overwhelming nor ultimately decisive. And the television news bulletin seems to confirm that view. For if it makes us witnesses of many of the world's agonies, it also gives us glimpses of its glories. The news that exposes us to wounds being inflicted also shows them being bound up. We see not just parched deserts being endured but also cups of water being proffered. Pictures that make us shudder at natural calamity sometimes humble us before the sheer goodness and self-sacrifice of the human response.

We rarely see raw evil depicted in television news, evil out of control, on the rampage. The context is invariably one of challenge and response — gruesome road accident *and* ambulance crews treating casualties; plane crash *and* rescue workers painstakingly picking their way through the wreckage; distraught relatives of violence victims *and* friends and neighbours comforting them.

That parable Jesus told about the wheat and the weeds is bang up to the minute. Wheat and weeds, symbolizing good and evil, grow together in a field, inextricable, nurtured by the same sun, watered by the same rain, woven together to the point where you cannot pick up a handful of one without strands of the other being included. Until the harvest, that is. The television news bulletin is a vivid commentary on that parable – morally ambiguous life in history's field this side of the harvest.

In a curious way, although television news depicts evil extensively, it also puts it in its place, subdues it within a fixed time-frame as though to say: "We are not going to allow ourselves to be overwhelmed by this awful carry-on in the world. We mark it and feel its impact, but we will not become obsessed by it."

This unwillingness to permit the grisly side of life to dominate the rest does not make the reality any easier to bear for those enduring it, but it does offer reassurance to the others. The strict time-discipline of the television news signifies the truth that we may have to peep over the edge into the black chasm from which human wickedness and natural calamity bubble up, but we don't have to make a full-time career of it, like witches round a perpetually simmering cauldron. Instead we shall make a cup of tea and get on with the business of normal living.

Such an attitude could be called purblind complacency or sheer escapism, but that is the way human beings have survived and kept their sanity from the dawn of history – by averting their eyes from the surrounding darkness and concentrating on the cheerful flames of the fire.

And there is this much to be said about the rigorous view of life we derive from television news bulletins. At least we know that what we have seen is the sum of the most significant things that might do harm to us and to our personal world. We can be reasonably sure that no greater catastrophe is being kept hidden from us because

television news editors have decided we haven't the
stomach for it.

Should viewers get the idea in their heads that, for
whatever sinister or compassionate motives, unpalatable
truths are being left out of bulletins, then the credibility
of television news as a reliable information service would
be fatally undermined. One conviction that reputable television journalists have burned into their souls is this: as a
general rule items should never be left out of a news
bulletin because of the effect they might have on those at
the receiving end.

This was the ground over which the "other battle" of
the Falklands raged. The BBC and ITN came under heavy
fire from politicians for showing footage of the suffering
of British service men and women which was judged to
be sapping of the national morale. But another of the
parables of Jesus is relevant here – the one about the house
being swept clean of one devil and left empty to be invaded
by seven more. The suppression of bad news does not
make the public more prone to think happy thoughts.
They don't believe they are any safer in an Eden where
bird songs are magnified in order to drown out the ser-
pent's hiss. Human curiosity, like nature, abhors a
vacuum; in the absence of hard intelligence it will be filled
with rumour, speculation and all the fevered imaginings
of people's worst fears.

The World Our Parish

It cannot be denied that the world is a saner, happier,
more law-abiding place than a casual glance at a television
news bulletin might suggest. But that is a case the television output as a whole must argue. A twenty-minute

news bulletin cannot be expected to offer a comprehensive account of the state of the world.

We are unfair to television journalists when we load on them the whole burden of proving that life is worth living, and then give them only thirty minutes three times a day to do it. Indeed, when journalists ill-advisedly assume the role of Cheerful Chappies and start adding a statutory proportion of happy stories to their bulletins for therapeutic reasons, we just don't believe them. "Must be short of news tonight!", we snort, as we watch a budgerigar riding a miniature bicycle along a clothes line or listen to the shock-horror disclosure that Princess Diana has changed her hair stylist.

Viewers are not convinced by Mickey Mouse stories planted in the news to raise their spirits, because they know from personal experience that whatever the theologians may say about the world being a good creation, it's a deadly dangerous place through which to negotiate one's way.

Indeed, the public's lust for news originates in a sense of psychic insecurity. Our forebears probably felt more at home in the world than we do, because it was a much more circumscribed cosmos than ours. Unless they were unlucky enough to be living in the eye of the hurricane, happenings way beyond the parish boundary were already merging into history by the time they heard of them. Now, to paraphrase John Wesley's words, the whole world is our parish. No part of it is truly remote as the intercontinental ballistic missile flies or the New York stock exchange fluctuates or the Russian grain harvest flourishes or fails. Cast across our lives is a great spider's web of interlocking forces held in delicate equilibrium – a balance capable of being disrupted at any moment.

This may always have been the case, but now we *know* it, almost instantaneously. The speed of modern communication, besides being a most powerful engine of cultural and social change, also keeps us in a state of psychic turmoil. We need to be assured, frequently, that things are holding together in those parts of the big world that could affect our little world. So let's put the news on.

And yet there's a credit side to all this. We viewers are dignified by being invited to share the concerns of a big world – a compliment we might prefer to shrug off, given our natural insularity. When I proposed earlier that the theme of the news is things which might affect me and my little world, I was giving television journalists less than their due. They seek to push back the frontiers of that little world. Because of their efforts, it is a bigger, wider world that bursts into my sitting-room.

Those who construct television news bulletins know what will directly concern and intrigue me. And they know this, not just because they are clever technicians but because they share the same environment. They too are workers, parents, city dwellers fearful of mugging, car drivers nervous about motorway madness, citizens of the nuclear age living in a prime target, threatened by unemployment, worried about the quality of health care or the standard of public education.

Television journalists have little difficulty in engaging with me at the point of my primary concerns. But they also try to do something much harder and confront me with the answers to questions I am not asking. This is the nature of all journalism, of course. Journalists cannot afford to be insular; they scan a more expansive horizon than mine, have a wider range of concerns, trace the complex filaments of my life away into the distance, see connections between this and that which would never occur to me. It's a hit-and-miss business for them. If they miss, the bulletin was a bore, a switch-off, full of foreign stories of no possible interest. If they hit the mark, I become just a tiny bit more of a citizen of the world than I was before.

True Deceivers

I suppose it all boils down to the question: can we trust the television journalists? You will gather that I have much respect for them. Their strengths and weaknesses have been the subject of sustained academic analysis and public debate. The more perceptive of them genially concede the predispositions of their trade, some of which I've already mentioned – the tendency to follow the visual imperative, letting the quality of the pictures determine the worth of the story; the addiction to the cult of the "new" for its own sake; the assumption that they can record the dilemmas, conflicts and divisions of society without sharing them, as though the television newsroom were a demilitarized zone rather than one more battle-ground; their under-estimation of the extent to which the things which belong to their humanness – matters of culture, education, class and sex – colour their editorial judgements.

All this is just saying that, like the rest of us, journalists are miserable sinners operating in a morally ambiguous world, trying to do the impossible: tell the precise truth using very imprecise tools. Television news certainly offers us refracted images of the world. But then, every representation of the truth has a statutory proportion of distortion in it. No one knows this better than the theologian, pledged to mediate mysterious reality by way of the crude and inexact disciplines of language.

In one of his letters, Paul calls Christians "true

deceivers". Presumably he meant that, in a warped world, exact truth can only be expressed through symbols which involve a certain degree of deception – as when an artist uses perspective to suggest that parallel rows of houses meet at the horizon. It is deception in the interests of the truth, sometimes at the expense of literal fact.

In this sense, television journalists have no option but to be "true deceivers". They are trying to make sense of experience, and if experience were transparent in meaning and could be dissolved without remainder in images and words, we would be infallible. Reflection, judgement, opinion would become redundant human preoccupations. So would faith, since it makes no sense to take someone or something on trust when we *know* beyond a shadow of a doubt. It is in the metaphysical wilderness between symbol and reality that all purveyors of truth, whether theologians or journalists, are doomed to wander.

In the Book of Genesis, it is God who brings order out of chaos; in the world of the mass media, it is these true deceivers, television news editors. They subdue into harmony a mountain of telex print-outs, miles of video tape and a pandemonium of ringing telephones. They organize into a coherent picture a riot of impressions, a chaos of events, a bedlam of attitudes and opinions that would otherwise have us scurrying to the hills in a panic. They offer us a view of the world we can live with.

And this is a world view that does not emerge from endless reflection in the groves of Academe. Aristotle had no six o'clock deadline to meet. Journalists have to put their version of events together at lightning speed, in a welter of almost instantaneous judgements. And I want to suggest in all seriousness that this work of putting a frame round our experience is a religious service in the strictest meaning of the word. For is not the word "religion" derived from the Latin root, "religiare", to tie together or to bind? And is not this what the television journalist does when he or she knits together verbal and visual symbols into some semblance of reality?

This television version of reality is distorted, incomplete and never, thank God, beyond challenge, for in a democracy no single account of the truth is sovereign. Television journalists sell their wares in a public market place, with rival stall-holders on all sides bellowing their competing versions. No single source of news has exclusive access to the public ear and eye, though some are more seductive than others. There is balancing power in the multiplicity of news media, in competing channels and even in the variety of perceptions on offer within the same broadcasting organization.

Now, Christians should be accustomed to this synoptic or summary view of the truth. That's after all why we call the first three gospels synoptic, because they offer parallel but by no means identical accounts of the same story.

In one of his regular columns for the *Daily News*, long before the birth of broadcasting, G. K. Chesterton wrote: "The pedantic decisions and definable readjustments of man may be found in scrolls and statute books and scriptures; but man's basic assumptions and everlasting energies are to be found in penny dreadfuls and halfpenny novelettes." He might allow me to amplify the quotation by adding that it is from popular journalism, especially in its most vivid, pictorial forms, that believers can quarry a rich seam of parable, discover the raw stuff of their theologizing, and receive a salutary jolt to any sentimental half-baked notions of how God deals with the world.

It is the news which drives most believers, with particular urgency, to penitence and intercession, because it thrusts at them in stark and up-to-the-minute form the perennial questions about meaning, destiny and purpose.

That's just a pompous way of saying that the news is the first rough draft of history, and the believer has the task of trying to make sense of it.

SIX

THE DEAD TOO HAVE THEIR RIGHTS

On 30th January 1986 the U.S. space shuttle *Challenger* disintegrated in mid-air shortly after take-off. Its end was witnessed live on television by hundreds of millions of viewers. The seven astronauts probably died the most public deaths in the history of the world. So spectacular were the television pictures of *Challenger* blowing apart that they were shown repeatedly over the next few days.

We saw it once, that awesome, deadly cloud which incinerated seven human beings in the blink of an eye, then we saw it again, and again and again. To die out of due time, watched by hundreds of millions of spectators, violates some ultimate right to privacy, but it could be regarded as just bad luck – the cameras happened to be on the spot and running. But to die repeatedly as a matter of public record turns one's end into a form of spectator sport, like a public execution or one of those death-defying circus stunts that go wrong and justify the high admission fee.

Those of a religious turn of mind were no doubt awed by *Challenger*'s apocalyptic end, as seven souls left time for eternity before their eyes. Humanists could hardly have been less disconcerted. The billions of years of evolutionary pain that went into the making of Commander Scobee and his crew were negated in a blinding flash; a dramatic symbol of a wasteful universe.

Either way, the world witnessed the ultimate event in the lives of the *Challenger* seven, and will see it again and again because these deaths on the frontier of space are unrepeatable moments, like Roger Bannister's four-minute mile or the ascent of Everest by Hillary and Tensing. They can happen only once in history, and must therefore be celebrated periodically as high solemn moments in the history of the tribe.

The first showing of the end of *Challenger* was news of great importance. The second time we saw it, we were given the opportunity, of which shock robbed us the first time round, to reflect on the bravery of the astronauts and the price that must be paid if we are to become citizens of the universe. But from then on, with each showing of the fireball that became a shroud, news gradually degenerated into newszak.

Newszak.[11] *Challenger* vapourizing in a puff of pretty white smoke now takes its place on that endlessly replayed and replayable tape, alongside footage of John F. Kennedy in Dallas putting his hand up to his head and his wife staring incredulously at her blood-spattered dress: and the record of the moment Donald Campbell's *Bluebird* launched itself like a guided missile from the surface of Lake Windermere: and that scratchy film of the airship *Hindenberg*, about to tie up in New York, suddenly becoming a glowing, skeletal lantern and crumpling like charred paper to the ground.

Newszak is to news what muzak is to music. Muzak is all that is left of music when its performance ceases to be an occasion and becomes a background, an interminable flood of sound, fitfully recognizable, that floats in and out of our consciousness. Muzak is the husk of music, what remains after its emotional power has been discharged. It is still serviceable in a society which cannot stand or is not allowed to have silence.

Newszak is the husk of news – events drained of topicality, moments evacuated of their original horror, splendour or interest, sensations that have lost the sting of their first impact but still make pretty or shocking pictures like embellishments on an ancient tomb. Newszak offers evocative images for every occasion to jolt the viewer into attention. It is the visual equivalent of Pavlov's bell which stirs psychologically conditioned animals to slaver for their next meal.

There are occasions when it is entirely appropriate that the fiery end of *Challenger* should be shown again, but it is as newszak that the footage will offer an easy way out for film makers casting around for shocking images to point up lesser truths than the original event signified. Newszak is an electronic junk yard where bits and pieces can always be found to titivate any producer's old jalopy of a programme.

It could be argued that television, like any other art form, is entitled to re-run its epic moments. After all, Mozart's music was not composed to be played only once, and the ceiling of the Sistine Chapel was not painted to be admired for a couple of Sundays and then rubbed clean like a blackboard. But when the content of newszak is someone's real-life death, then all the rules change, because this is an ultimate taboo we are flouting. From time immemorial, taboos have been one of society's defences against moral decay and spiritual darkness, and are not to be shrugged off carelessly.

The average citizen dies once, usually off-screen. The

illustrious dead, like John F. Kennedy and the *Challenger* seven, will die and die and die again. Critics say that television, because of its intrusiveness, is rough on the living. If so, it is utterly merciless on the dead. There is no need to get them to sign release forms for their pictures to be used. After a plane crash, the dead lie in neat white bundles, some ominously abbreviated; or rest under police tarpaulins, the scene of their death agony marked out by tape. And from faraway places, where we need not be so punctilious because there are no relatives to complain to MPs or to the Broadcasting Complaints Commission, the dead lie hideously exposed, denied the grace of privacy.

Death on television confronts journalists with an age-old problem in stark new forms. The forbidden sights that modern society is busy hiding away behind hospital bed screens are imploding into viewers' sitting-rooms.

Our forebears confronted death as a common daily occurrence. So now do we. But we don't have the theological framework – if that is not too portentous a phrase for the melange of liturgy, hymnody, faith, superstition and folk wisdom – which enabled them to make sense of death.

It is neither possible nor desirable that television should become an electronic version of the original *Christian Science Monitor* which, it is alleged, firmly excluded death, disaster, illness, unhappiness and general mayhem from its columns. In which case, there needs to be a much clearer recognition and conscious acknowledgement that the dead, too, have their rights – to dignity, to privacy, to freedom from the endless enactment for ulterior purposes of the moment of their passing.

The old rubrics referred to the "sacred" dead, to signify that this was a mystery in whose presence one should tread with care. Those who die under the merciless eye of the television camera deserve to be laid decently to rest and not relegated to newszak's junk yard for spare-person surgery in some television cutting room.

The Public's "Right to Know"

Challenger's flaming end on television is a specific instance of a much wider issue. Television has made dramatic inroads into areas of life traditionally regarded as off-limits to public scrutiny. The medium is no more intrusive than what is euphemistically called investigative journalism, but because it is a live medium and deals in pictures which are more dramatic and revealing than words, and because a greater proportion of the population watches a major TV channel than reads any one newspaper, the cumulative effect can be devastating.

This erosion of the boundary between the private and public domains of life is justified by all the media on the grounds that the public has "the right to know".[12] Given the almost paranoid tendency of most governments to cultivate secrecy for its own sake, the public undoubtedly has a right to know many more things than it is told. But there is great danger in elevating "the public's right to know" into a philosophical principle which can be used to justify virtually *any* disclosure.

The 1973 Code of Ethics of U.S. Journalists states that "The public's right to know of events of public importance and interest is the over-riding mission of the mass media" and "journalists must be free of obligations to any interest other than the public's right to know". It is worth asking the question: what kind of a right, precisely, is the public's "right to know"? Given the almost limitless range of human knowledge, the public's "right" to it is as unenforceable as a claim to own property on Mars. A right which cannot be exercised has little other than the force of rhetoric. Nor can the public have a general *legal* right to know the truth, otherwise those in possession of it would have a *legal* duty to disclose it.

As a matter of natural justice, the public at large has no right to know all kinds of things any individual knows; otherwise he or she has no identity, no proper boundary between the self and others. Hence, neither broadcasters nor journalists can justify the indiscriminate disclosure of information by appealing to some general principle that the public has a right to know. There has got to be some morally defensible reason for spilling the beans.

Two specific inhibitions on the public's right to know are secrecy and privacy; and the issue is needlessly complicated because the two terms are often used interchangeably when in fact they refer to distinct conditions that lay different moral obligations on broadcasters. The core of secrecy is intentional concealment; the essence of privacy is deliberate exclusion.

Secrecy, as its Latin root suggests, is the setting apart from the common store of knowledge certain lore whose restricted possession constitutes power and whose loss would result in vulnerability. Privacy is actually or metaphorically a territorial right; the claim to a personal domain from which the public is kept out.

There are good reasons why journalists may, within the limits of professional ethics, probe the boundaries of secrecy. For instance, when the presumption is that the Government is improperly withholding knowledge that really belongs to the public – matters to do with their welfare and safety. The public has a right to know that a make of car is unsafe, or that certain types of high-rise flats are fire-risks, or that smoking causes disease, and so

111

on and on. Since the public has no way of deciding whether such secrecy is justified, because not only the contents of the secrets but their very existence is shrouded in obscurity, the journalist has a right to ferret out the truth. For as Lord Acton wrote, "Everything secret degenerates; nothing is safe that does not show how it can bear discussion and publicity."

Privacy is a different matter. In the end, unlike secrecy, it is not bound up with what one possesses but with who one is. It safeguards personal identity, the distinction between I and Not-I. Every human being therefore is entitled to some inviolate inner sanctum to which no one else has access except by invitation. And Christians would derive this right neither from the law nor from morality but from the biblical doctrine of man.

Even those who use their privacy as a cloak for illegal or anti-social activities do not lose their right to all of it when they are exposed. The pornographer or drug-dealer may forfeit the right to privacy in the matter of his bank account but not in his dealings with his children. Nobody, however degenerate or evil, can be reduced to the status of a non-person by having every shred of privacy torn away.

All this suggests a rule which has a bearing on the *Challenger* episode. Since broadcasters and journalists operate within the public domain, they can only enter a private realm with the express permission of those who occupy it. The launch and explosion of the space shuttle was a public event; the incomprehension, horror and grief on the faces of the watching relatives was not. If people are in no position to give consent for microphones or cameras to penetrate their private space, it must be assumed that they have withheld that permission.

The Dead Too Have Their Rights

The dead and the unconscious, those in deep shock or incapacitated by grief, the mentally impaired and children have no way of deciding whether or not they wish to give up their right to privacy. Their silence must not be taken for tacit approval. Unless there is an over-riding humanitarian interest immediately apparent to all who see the pictures or hear the programme, those who cannot defend their privacy must not be subjected to an act of force masquerading as the public's right to know.

The dead are the limiting case. They do not forfeit the right to privacy because they are in no position to assert it. Since they cannot preserve their own dignity or hide their awful helplessness, it is the duty of the living to protect them.

The general public sense this, which is why they get particularly angry about intrusive cameras at funerals. Most people are both embarrassed and upset at having to watch the grief of others. Because all must die, and most human beings suffer bereavement at one time or another, this is an area of acute sensitivity. Some funerals are properly a matter of public record at which the presence of discreetly handled cameras is appropriate – as when the dead person has been in the public eye for some reason, or the funeral is more than a private occasion because it focuses national or community or political sentiment. But every funeral is a corporate gathering at which the rubrics for the burial of the deal leave space for intensely personal and private rites of parting.

Cameras may register the fact that a funeral is taking place and give an impression of its dimensions, but they have no more right to subject grief-stricken mourners to close scrutiny than they would have to burst in on the death-bed scene in the first place. The bereaved need to vent their grief in whatever way they feel appropriate, otherwise they may suffer psychological damage. The presence of prying cameras must distort this process, either by impelling mourners to put a brave face on things or by forcing them to express grief with unnatural emotion, lest the public think they did not care sufficiently for the one who has died.

The verbal equivalent of the intrusive camera in its invasion of a person's private space is the question directed at the distressed, "How do you feel?" It is an impertinent enquiry because it forces anguished people to try to put their emotions into words long before they are in a state to do so; it is hypocritical because the interviewer or reporter is not primarily concerned with the subject's welfare but with obtaining some disclosure for the benefit of eavesdroppers, and it is professionally incompetent because it is a clichéd and lazy way of getting a "moving" interview.

All in all the handling of privacy is a supreme test of the broadcaster's maturity of judgement, not just as a technician but as a human being. And the crux of the matter is the way he or she deals with the right to privacy of those who are in no position to complain. The necessary gift is best described by that antique but lovely word "charity" – the same impulse that would have us clothe the naked and bind up the wounds of the broken also impels us to show magnanimity to those being humiliated through exposure to the public gaze.

There is also another human gift involved – discretion, both in its conventional meaning as care for good manners and in the stronger sense of intuitive ability to navigate between the private and shared worlds of people, and to know what properly belongs to each. The quality of being able to recognize the psychological and moral boundaries between people is known as "tact" – a word which conveys the physical sense of touching that these boundaries evoke.

Even in secular society we refer to the "holy" dead, acknowledging that there is still a realm whose integrity must be protected from indiscriminate public gaze, for there dwells the sacred. Careless disclosure of such things is, literally, shameful.

SEVEN

WOUNDED BY
A GHOST

"Oh, what a blow that phantom gave me" – the quotation is taken from Cervantes' *Don Quixote* and was used by Edmund Carpenter as the title of an important paperback on the impact of the media on culture. But to me, the image is also evocative of one of the most tantalizing and clamant of contemporary social problems, that of violence on television – whose ghostly images, it is claimed, are capable of reaching out from the screen and doing us damage in real life.

Without doubt, the issue of violence on television is very high on the public agenda at the present time – church assemblies have been passing resolutions and newspaper leaders pontificating, Parliamentarians demanding action and broadcasters responding with research reports, seminars and tougher guide-lines. The British government's concern and its unwillingness to allow the BBC and ITV to keep or put their own houses in order has been reflected in the creation of a new statutory body, the Broadcasting Standards Council, one of whose main tasks is to monitor the levels of violence on television.

The assertion that there is too much violence on television has become as much a part of contemporary folk wisdom as "Britain is being swamped by black immigrants" or "The BBC is run by trendy left-wingers". The weight of evidence for such opinions, or lack of it, has no effect upon the tenacity with which they are held. In the case of television violence, mountains of research reports warning against simplistic conclusions are blown away in gusts of fury by moralists appalled at the state of our society and casting around for the source of the depravity. Lo and behold, they discern its glassy eye staring at them from the corner of their living-rooms.

This is not to suggest that public rumblings about television violence should be discounted by broadcasters. It is scant reassurance that there are few telephone calls of protest about television violence. The Civil Aviation Authority reports that every year it gets fewer complaints about aircraft noise from people living under Heathrow's flight path. This is not because aircraft have got quieter but because the residents have gone deafer, slowly conditioned to accept bedlam as normality. People ingesting small amounts of asbestos dust or absorbing low doses of radiation over long periods of time usually find little to complain about in the early stages either.

There clearly *is* a problem here, but it is much more complex than the sterner critics of television will allow. They are setting terms for the current debate that parody a diffuse and ethically ambiguous issue to which few of us have given sufficient thought. And for those who attempt to look at great issues through the eyes of faith, it is not a headache just for Christians who work in the media. The core of the issue is located not on the television screen but at the heart of our society, where there is obviously a moral and social vacuum that television obligingly fills. And honesty requires one to confess that the churches aren't making much of a fist at filling that vacuum themselves.

What follows, therefore, is an attempt to use television violence as a lens through which to look at the nature of contemporary society — over which God is sovereign and for which Christ died. Our theology of mission must take account of this many-faceted phenomenon, some manifestations of which cannot be laid at the door of broadcasters in particular or fallen human nature in general. They must be attributed to what the old insurance policies quaintly called Acts of God.

What is Violence?
What have these in common — a Tom and Jerry cartoon, news footage of the Mexico City earthquake, Carmen being stabbed in Bizet's opera, the space shuttle tragedy, Angie's attempted suicide in *East Enders*, a burst of profanity from a frustrated football supporter, an African lion bringing down a gazelle, and Terry Wogan kicking a teddy bear in his chat show? They all figured in a catalogue of "unacceptably" violent incidents on television compiled by a national newspaper anxious to protect its more sensitive readers from shocking pictures — other than those contained within its own pages, of course.

On the other hand, a survey report compiled in 1972 by Professor R. Blumenthal called *Justifying Violence; Attitudes of American Men* found that over 30 per cent of a national sample of American males did not regard the police beating-up students as an act of violence, and 57 per cent took the same view about police shooting looters. Using napalm against Vietnamese villagers was similarly viewed. Evidently, violence is what They do to Us. We apply discipline to enforce law and order upon Them, but that isn't violence.

So the debate about television violence is bedevilled

from the start by problems of definition. Given the wide variety of human response to the same stimulus – what gives one pleasure frightens another – if all the images reported to have shocked susceptible viewers were aggregated and banished from television screens, the schedules would contain little other than the epilogue, the weather forecast on a calm day, and gardening programmes purged of distressing footage of voracious caterpillars savaging harmless plants.

The problem is: where does any definition of television violence stop? Restrict it to hurting human beings and you rouse the sleeping tiger in animal lovers – what about bull fighting or even fox hunting? So they demand that the definition cover all higher forms of life. This arouses the ire of conservationists who insist that *all* life is sacred – to swat a fly is to do violence to nature. But even if the definition is extended to all forms of life, this will not satisfy those doughty capitalists who regard damage to property as only marginally less heinous than mass murder. After all, it was not that long ago that you could be hanged for stealing a loaf of bread but merely transported to the colonies for beating a child to death.

Then there is the violence for which no human agency is responsible – those natural catastrophes such as earthquake, flood, volcanic eruption, hurricane and drought. They do immense damage to life and property and produce shocking pictures, but can they be classified with, say, acts of grievous bodily harm in a television crime series, as though God were the Great Mugger in the Sky?

Nor is there any way forward in relying on some kind of public consensus. For *the* public does not exist. There are as many publics as there are interests, preoccupations and passions in human nature. Which television public should we use as our standard for acceptable TV violence? There is on the one hand the public represented by The National Viewers' and Listeners' Association, which finds *East Enders* offensive, and on the other the public, twenty-four million strong, that watches it avidly every week. There is the public represented by the handful of calls protesting at gratuitous violence in some late-night film, and the more vociferous public who complain that the most violent bits have been cut out of it.

People are strangely schizoid about the violence issue. Without any sense of incongruity, they will watch and presumably enjoy violent programmes, and still go on record as insisting that "the" public needs protecting from that kind of thing. "The" public seems to be a fragile, highly moral abstraction upon whom we lay the vulnerabilities from which we exempt ourselves. This element of double-think may go far to explain the confused nature of many of the research findings about television violence.

But *the* public is an unreliable guide to what is acceptable for a more fundamental reason. Not to put too fine a point on it, many people love violence; they are morbidly fascinated by it. So they congregate at the scene of a road accident, or in their tens of millions watch medical programmes like *Your Life in Their Hands* where surgeons hack patients about in full view of technicolour cameras. Violence has always been a central strain in popular culture; and in classical culture too. Eviscerate the Bible or Greek tragedy or Shakespeare of all violence, and they would be in tatters.

The lure of violence may have something to do with the thrill of seeing breached a taboo about the inviolate nature of the human body. Possibly lurking beneath the layers of shock and even disgust when we observe acts of violence, is a ghastly sense of reassurance; their sheer awfulness points up by contrast our own good fortune. It is like the release of psychological tension after a funeral – partly secret, shame-faced relief that we are still alive.

Of course, we do not easily own up to harbouring such appalling feelings, but as Edmund Burke wrote, "I am convinced that we have a degree of delight, and that no small one, in the real misfortunes and pains of others." If there is even a tincture of truth in this theory, then those moralists who demand the wiping clean of the television screens would be inviting rioting in the streets if they got their way, because a key theme of popular culture had been obliterated from the air waves. And whatever else the public pay their licence fee for, it is certainly to see popular culture amply represented on television.

Some people insist that, even at midnight, programmes which might shock a five-year-old child who happened to be awake and in the vicinity of a television screen ought not to be transmitted. Such uncompromising moral rigour is admirable but demands not so much modifications of broadcasting policy as amendment of human nature. And in a secular society, that is the Church's or the preacher's job, not the broadcaster's. The harsh reality is that thirty million adults do not pay licence fees in order to be restricted to television programmes suited to small children.

Righteous Rhetoric

Though the general public is ambivalent about violence on television, and the research findings about its effects on the real world are totally inconclusive, the politicians are in no doubt about its baleful consequences. They have been much heard, directing stern admonitions at the broadcasters to put their house in order and demanding tougher media laws. Some MPs have given special attention to broadcasting and are making an important contribution to the debate about its future; others recognize television violence as an emotive issue which lends itself to highly moralistic rhetoric – but their comments say as much about the health of the body politic as about the medium.

It is, after all, a venerable tradition to blame communications technology for social disruption. A clear historical line joins the decapitation of the bearers of bad news in ancient Greece and the exclusion of television crews from black townships in South Africa. And the invention of printing, which encouraged pamphleteering, was held responsible for the upsurge of militant nationalism in Europe.

A famous *Times* leader ran: "Before the children's greedy eyes, with heartless indiscrimination, are presented night after night terrific massacres, horrible catastrophes. All who care for the moral well-being and education of the child will set their faces like flint against this form of excitement." This "form of excitement" was not *East Enders* or a Clint Eastwood western, but the invention of cinematography. The leader was dated twelfth April 1913. And according to Marshall McLuhan, the arrival of the first comic books on the American scene in 1935 was blamed for rising crime statistics. As he put it, "The dimmest-witted convict learned to plead from the dock, 'It wuz comic books what made me do it, M'Lud!'"

Politicians rarely find congenial the media's account of their policies. During the First World War, an edict went out prohibiting artists from depicting corpses. At the height of the trench war, the censors on both sides saw to it that not a single photograph or drawing of a dead soldier was published in any newspaper in Britain, France or Germany.

In a society characterized by growing unrest and alienation, violence can mean many things – the language of those who feel excluded and can find no other way of making their voices heard, or the argot of those driven by envy, hatred or sheer wickedness. Whatever the explanation, one official reaction is the urge to blot out the images of disaffection, to sanitize the television screen.

At any one time, a number of issues compete for the limited resources of government attention, most of which are, if not insoluble, then of such long-term significance as to offer little pay-off in public relations. But any issue which has a high public profile, is not too technical, and lends itself to powerful rhetoric will get special priority. Television violence is such an issue, and one which is counterpointed by real-life crises such as the day in the town of Hungerford when a killer ran riot. Then the public demands firm action. Demands for the banning of sniper films on television were an evocative way of registering official concern, even though the Hungerford killer apparently fed his fantasy life on videos and gun magazines rather than television.

The Case Against Violence

If we leave to one side the scruples of those who find violence ugly, and for aesthetic reasons would rather not see it on their screens, or timid viewers who are upset and frightened by it and don't want to be reminded that such things go on in the world, what are the main moral arguments for cutting back radically on television violence?

There is the copy-cat argument. Viewers, particularly young people, will be incited by what they see on television to repeat the same behaviour on the streets. This is the correlation that research scientists all over the world have been seeking in literally thousands of studies and experiments. And in vain. When a slight correlation between habitual watching of violent television programmes and aggressive behaviour has been established, no one can distinguish the chicken from the egg. Does watching violent television produce the aggression, or is it that aggressive people particularly choose to watch violent programmes?

Or is there a third factor which causes both phenomena? For instance, in copy-cat violence, which cat is being copied? If someone watches on television a husband murder his wife by dropping an electric fire in her bath, and then the next morning disposes of her by the same method, it could be argued that television showed him how to give vent to his homicidal tendencies. But there is no evidence that television instilled those homicidal instincts into him in the first place. Before the days of television, Agatha Christie novels offered a potential villain a dozen ingenious ways of getting rid of an unwanted relative. But no one cried, "Ban Agatha Christie!"

It would be foolish to under-estimate the extent to which television might promote the notion of violence as a neat problem-solving device, but the crude terms in which the copy-cat argument is employed take no account of the complexities of human behaviour. Common sense rather than social theory suggests that society is such an infinitely elaborate system of interlocking forces, pressures and relationships, that there is no simple, single cause of *any* social ill.

And the copy-cat argument must work both ways. If viewers ought to fear copy-cat violence, ought they to be encouraged by copy-cat virtue? Some critics allege that the BBC's soap opera *East Enders* sets a bad example to young people because drug trafficking, blackmail and illegitimacy feature in its plots. But much more of its screen time is taken up with the themes of family solidarity, racial tolerance, the care of the elderly, battles to save a stormy marriage, and a host of other wholesome virtues earthed in a totally believable community with its fair share of human wickedness and fallibility. It is a modern morality play and as such very much on the side of the angels, even though Old Nick makes an appearance from time to time.

There is also the argument that television violence desensitizes viewers to the point where they take acts of brutality for granted. Television viewers are no different from medical students who feel queasy the first time they confront a cadaver but within weeks are eating their sandwiches off the dissecting table. Sustained doses of any stimulus have a numbing effect, which is the nub of the case – but with an important qualification. Acts of violence on the small screen desensitize viewers to violence *on television* – the viewer's attitude to violence is distorted because the medium cannot engage all the senses central to the experience.

It is possible to show an act of violence on television but not to convey the pain. If scientists ever get around to marketing the "feelies" of Aldous Huxley's *Brave New World*, where television viewers in a surreal world experience the full sensuous impact of what they see, nine-tenths of fictional violence would vanish from the screen overnight. Who would want to pay *that* price for realism? The great count against gratuitous television violence is not so much that it desensitizes viewers as that it seriously misleads them about the nature of violence in the real world.

The young fed on a diet of television violence from an early age may come to believe that is the way the world is; violence seems a neat and efficient problem-solving device, and one that is comparatively painless.

Responsible programme makers are not just concerned with keeping gratuitous violence off the screen but also, paradoxically, with ensuring that the full impact of any legitimate violence is not played down. If, say, in a cop thriller, the villain who is thrown through the windscreen of a car gets up, cut and bruised, to carry on the action – that is the irresponsible use of violence because it is not violent enough. In real life, people who get thrown through car windscreens are either killed or grievously injured, and to give any other impression is seriously misleading about the nature of the world.

Yet even here, any simple relation of cause and effect is ruled out because television violence can under some conditions produce the opposite effect from desensitization. Violent news footage of drought or starvation may evoke waves of compassion, shame and the desire to be humanely useful. Or television violence may have a deterrent effect. The plays *Threads* and *The War Game* spared viewers nothing of the horrors of a nuclear explosion, but it is doubtful whether many of those who watched were spurred on to join the Society for the Propagation and Detonation of Hydrogen Bombs. The Campaign for Nuclear Disarmament probably did very well out of the two films.

Or consider the gruesome archive footage of First World War trench battles transmitted every year around Remembrance Sunday. There has never yet been a single complaint about gratuitous violence then on television. It is as though the elegiac context in which the violence is shown transforms it from a brutalizing to a piteous experience.

By far the most violent series in the history of television was undoubtedly Jeremy Isaac's epic twenty-four-part compilation of archive material, *The World at War*. Every permutation and combination of man's inhumanity to man was shown in all its horror, but it is safe to assume that the overall impression left on the average viewer by the harrowing footage was a noble and uplifting one to do with the triumph of the human spirit over demonic savagery.

Whilst it is pointless to pretend that what people see on television has no impact on their daily lives – ITV commercials are a billion-pound monument to the fact that people's spending patterns are changed by television – yet virtually every ringing affirmation about television's impact on the real world dies the death by a thousand qualifications – to the frustration of researchers, the chagrin of moralists and the bemusement of programme makers.

Mutual Responsibility

It might help to bring some rationality into this messy and rather strident debate if the duties of the broadcasters were matched against those of the public generally, and especially those interest groups, such as the churches, who seek to raise the level of public moral discourse.

One conclusive piece of research which broadcasters need to take seriously disclosed that viewers show a complex awareness of the distinction between the real and the fantastic. They take in their stride the stylized patterns of violent action found in cartoons and cowboy films. Far from more violence being worse than less, a large number of deaths in a Western or a James Bond film contribute to an air of unreality. Put differently, the more the violent scenes on television approximate to real-life situations viewers might find themselves in, the greater their degree of anxiety.

This finding lays upon broadcasters the responsibility of ensuring that there is no blurring of the distinction between the real and the fantastic in the depiction of violence. Dr Bernard Williams, who chaired a Committee of Inquiry into Pornography, puts it this way, "Everything depends on the extent to which the audience is intended to see, or naturally does see, the action as part of their experience, or at any rate a simple extension of it, as opposed to seeing the action as controlled by an order of things markedly distinct from what goes on in the real world with which they are acquainted." Put at its crudest, the bloody extermination of a whole town by a Green Thing from Mars is perceived as harmless entertainment, whereas a realistic reconstruction on *Crimewatch* of a masked intruder breaking into an old lady's home is likely to fill elderly viewers with real fear.

It is therefore vitally important that broadcasters should signal clearly what is fantasy and what is fact. That form of documentary drama known in the trade as "faction" – which is the fictional reconstruction of a real-life event combining both drama and news footage – can blunt the viewer's capacity to discriminate between what is true and what is imaginary. Anything which weakens the viewer's hold on reality is subversive of the public good.

At root, this is a matter of good manners; the broadcaster's duty is to see that the public know what he or she is up to, and avoid playing games with them or wilfully deceiving them. It all boils down to the question: can we trust the broadcasters to render a true account of life, not just its factual aspects, but fiction as well, for fiction too has its own integrity?

If truthfulness, the avoidance of blurring reality and fantasy, is one task laid upon broadcasters in keeping violence on television within bounds, then the exercise of that artistic quality, reticence, is another. The ability to communicate experience without spelling it out, to coax the imagination of the viewer without battering it into submission by specific images, marks out the truly creative producer. He or she can use the oblique, the allusive, the metaphorical to emphasize the emotional impact of what is not actually seen. It is surely no accident that "explicit" is the word most often used by pornographers in advertising their wares.

Here again, the distinction between fact and fantasy becomes significant. Reticence may mean something different to the drama producer and the news editor. Drama is about conflict, human beings under stress and in emotional, psychological or physical danger. Great playwrights have always known how to use reticence as a creative tool, but the advent of television has made their task more complex. The drama of the past was primarily verbal, as for example in Shakespeare. But once action must be shown rather than spoken about, the difficulties multiply, for pictures convey a complex series of messages. It is not just the degree of overt violence in the plot which has to be assessed, but all the unintended side effects that creep into the action and may not become apparent until the filming is finished and the editing begins.

But at least the drama producer has time to reflect, to ponder the raw material and make any moral judgements at leisure. News editors have no such luxury. Violent pic-

tures from all over the world flood into the news room
for immediate transmission, and the editor must decide
there and then how much horror the viewers need see in
order to understand the issue. There is a constant tightrope
to walk between voyeurism on the one hand and sanitizing
the news out of existence on the other.

The process of news gathering gets more sophisticated
by the day. A whole galaxy of new technology based
on satellite communication makes the viewer an instant
spectator to violent happenings anywhere on earth. Even
on a quiet day at home, there is bound to be a war, disaster
or natural calamity somewhere beneath the footprint of
a satellite.

It is an academic question whether we live in a more
violent world than previous generations endured; the difficulty is that we are made witnesses to a greater proportion of such violence as does occur. Yet even here,
reticence plays a great role in the good news editor's judgement – though only if the public were able to view the
violent footage which wasn't transmitted could the extent
of that reticence be appreciated.

For every moralist who demands that the screens be
purged of such violent images, there is another who claims
that broadcasters have no moral right to shield viewers
from the full impact of the way the world really is. They
argue that only when the public is confronted with the
total horror of terrorist violence can the political will be
harnessed to deal with it effectively.

We are back to this issue of truthfulness again; the
blurring of the distinction between fact and fantasy.
Reality can be so purged of its more shocking images that
it slides into fantasy – then the television journalist is
deluding rather than enlightening the public. And that

raises a whole different set of ethical questions to do with propaganda, the selective use of the truth for ideological purposes – even if the ideology is as innocent as trying to avoid disturbing comfortable and happy homes with discordant intelligence from the outside world.

The public too have some responsibility for bringing rationality into the debate about television violence. The disturbing truth is that television has assumed an undue importance in our culture because other institutions have declined in significance. For instance, more and more young people depend on television to supply them with models of how other human beings behave in diverse circumstances because most of the alternative sources of role models have shrunk in importance – the family, the neighbourhood unit, the community of the work place and, of course, the churches.

The phrase, "There's too much violence on television" is often a form of code. It is shorthand for a whole welter of anxieties felt by some viewers about the power of television, its ability to seduce them, take them over, alter their life patterns, move, outrage and stir them up. They may not be objectively justified in assigning to television this god-like or demonic role, but that is how they feel. And they know of no other way of expressing their resentment than by focusing on television's more disturbing and violent images.

When family and community ties weaken, impressionable viewers have no corrective barriers between themselves and television as a national source of image-making. So, television's power is magnified in the same way that sound is amplified in a room empty of furniture. Therefore, if society allows television, by default, to become its moral tutor, to usurp the role of family, school and church, then society must not complain about the moral deficiencies in the lessons the medium teaches. Those images on the television screen, including the violent ones to which such exception is taken, are magnified in impact because they are filling a psychic vacuum left by the withering of other sources of image-making.

But the churches in particular have another important task which they are not discharging with any spectacular success. Many of the most violent images to be seen on the television screen relate not to any human agency but are the result of natural cataclysm such as earthquake, drought and flood, or of large-scale accidents – acts of God, as we would once have said. There is an irrationality about such catastrophes, especially when they can be seen live on television as they happen, which disturbs many viewers who make no claims to religious belief.

It is arguable that the main task of the Christian as social commentator confronted with television violence is not so much to demand its removal as to explain its significance. Theodicy is a word not much used these days. It describes that part of theology concerned to defend the goodness and omnipotence of God against objections arising from the existence of evil and suffering in the world. In the television age, this could become the crux of any relevant theology of Christian mission.

In sum, it is not the amount of violence on television but general moral confusion which is the nub of the issue. For the public have no right to expect from programme makers a moral clarity that is lacking in the rest of society. After all, where does the programme maker get a code of ethics from? Codes of practice and guidelines form an essential safety net, but they cannot teach anyone to walk the tightrope in the first place. Only society can do that.

And if it is a society which does not have one over-arching and totally commanding moral position, but has one group of moral certainties at odds with another group, how is the programme maker to arbitrate between them?

Given a combination of general moral confusion and the problem of evolving a satisfactory definition of violence at all, it is clear that no simple binding set of rules can be imposed on programme makers. The boundary between the allowable and the impermissible portrayal of violence on television is not a fixed line but an ill-defined area, such as is found in some parts of the world where you only realize that you have strayed over the frontier when someone starts shooting at you.

No restrictions, however rigorous, will satisfy the sterner critics. If broadcasters ban Clint Eastwood gunning down his opponents, they will be reviled for allowing Noddy to beat Big Ears over the head with a balloon on a stick. This is not to suggest that public concern is unfounded or can be shrugged off. Broadcasting does its share in shaping society, and if it does not do so by design, it will do it any way through inadvertence.

Television is, after all, only half a century old; comparatively little is known about its effects on human behaviour. For instance, might the lowering of one moral inhibition, to do with the viewer's toleration of violence, encourage collapse at other points of his psyche? Questions such as these are sufficiently worrying to impel broadcasting administrators and responsible producers to opt for caution rather than artistic freedom at any price.

Meanwhile, the core of wisdom will be found not in any rule book but in the body of practical decision-making that takes place in studios, film cutting rooms and locations where a thousand judgements a day have to be made on the spot about what is socially responsible and morally acceptable. The miracle is that, against increasing odds, these programme makers get it right sufficiently often for the rare exceptions to cause a public outcry.

But these judgements cannot be made in a vacuum, otherwise the programme makers will become increasingly remote from the public they are addressing. There has to be constant dialogue with all those bodies and individuals who care for the level of moral discourse in our society. But the qualification for taking part in that debate has got to be informed understanding of the complexities and dilemmas the programme makers face.

Neither moral generalizations nor swingeing anathemas are of much practical value to the film editor who has a mere five minutes to decide which snatches of the miles of stomach-churning film of, say, the Hillsborough football disaster, the public need to see in order to understand the scale of the tragedy. Artistic reticence on the programme maker's side must be balanced by reticence of judgement on the part of the moralists.

EIGHT

THE DEBATE ABOUT RELIGIOUS BROADCASTING

Do We Need It?

Religious broadcasting is always under threat from two directions. Firstly, there are those in the broadcasting industry, usually eager young products of a maturely secular society, who see religious broadcasting as a hang-over of the long gone Reithian era — along with radio announcers wearing full evening dress, Uncle Mac telling bedtime stories and nightly transmissions ending with the National Anthem.

These sceptics would insist that there has been a radical change in the religious temper of British society since the 1920s when John Reith, the first Director-General of the BBC, magisterially settled the issue of religious broadcasting by invoking the Monarch. The BBC must broadcast Christian programmes, he ruled, because the King was a Christian and therefore Christianity was the official religion of Britain. In the late 1980s, deepening secularization, multi-faith diversity and an ambiguous Christian situation suggest to the sceptics that the persistence of a broadcasting policy originally founded on the twin pillars of an appeal to the House of Windsor and Reith's Presbyterian zealotry is so bizarre as to be indefensible.

The new generation do not contest the fact that the sphere of religion throws up issues, events and personalities that must be taken account of, but argues that these could be dealt with in general programmes. The Annan Committee on the Future of Broadcasting, which reported in 1976, apparently agreed with this view. It said, "There is no reason why religion should not be present as an influence in all programmes, reminding the moralists of spiritual values and the social scientists of the inevitability of individual moral choice."

That sentence is significant for its description of religion as a combination of spiritual values and moral choices. The element most believers would regard as normative of religion – worship – is left out of account altogether. So it should be, say the young sceptics, for it was this Reithian obsession which turned the BBC into a crypto-church where, until the late 1960s, the Daily Service was introduced by an announcer who used the formula, "*Our* prayers are taken from . . . " – the implication being that "*We*, the BBC, are joining with you in this daily act of worship" – the Director-General kneeling by his desk, the commissionaire at the gate doffing his cap, the engineer on the far-flung transmitter moderating for fifteen minutes his salty language.

A distinguished former Head of Religious Broadcasting at the BBC unwittingly gave aid and succour to the secularizers when he told the Pilkington Committee in 1960 that "all television is religious television". This definition was brief, simple and comprehensive but was read by some as meaning that if religion was an underlying theme in all television programmes there was little need for a specialist department dedicated to the subject – which was not what he meant at all.

The second threat to religious broadcasting does not come from those who believe it is given more resources, prominence and protection than it deserves, but from quite a different direction – from the angle of faith rather than of scepticism. There are those who believe religion is too important to be subjected to the trivializing techniques endemic to broadcasting. Broadcasting, they insist, is just an art form; it is not a substitute for real life. There are certain areas of human experience into which the cameras and microphones ought not to pry. And one such sphere is that transaction between the human soul and God which we call religion.

Those who take this line are not necessarily Luddite in their attitude to inventions such as television. Indeed, they may well be impressed by the argument of Marshall McLuhan that the medium decisively changes the nature of the message. It may be genuine religion which enters the system at the camera end, but it is entertainment that emerges at the other, the domestic TV set. They argue that not all forms of discourse can be translated from one medium to another. A television screen is not a window through which the armchair worshipper can look in on religious worship and derive something of the same experience he or she might get from church attendance.

Neil Postman, Professor of Communications at New York University, states the case against television religion in this way:

Several characteristics of television and its surround converge to make authentic religious experience impossible. The first has to do with the fact that there is no way to consecrate the space in which a television show is experienced. It is an essential condition of any traditional religious service that the space in which it is conducted must be invested with some measure of sacrality. . . .

Moreover, the television screen itself has a strong bias toward a psychology of secularism. The screen is so saturated with our memories of profane events, so deeply associated with the commercial and entertainment worlds that it is difficult for it to be recreated for sacred events . . . the main message of the screen is a continual promise of entertainment. The television screen wants you to remember that its imagery is always available for your amusement and pleasure.[13]

Postman quotes the executive director of the American National Religious Broadcasters Association: "The unwritten law of all television preachers is that you can get your share of the audience only by offering people something they want." The concern of most great religious leaders, of course, has been to offer people what they need rather than what they want. But television is better suited to answering wants than to meeting needs. It is, in the jargon, "user-friendly". It does not accommodate complex language or stringent demands; it celebrates affluence and radiates good cheer.

Answering the claims of television evangelists that they can reach hundreds of millions of people with the Gospel in one telecast, Postman quotes Hannah Arendt to the effect that the danger of mass culture – trying to make *Hamlet* as entertaining as *My Fair Lady*, and *Songs of Praise* as glitzy as *Saturday Night at the Palladium* – is precisely that they may become very entertaining indeed. There are many great works of the past which have survived centuries of oblivion and neglect, but it is an open question whether they could survive entertaining versions of themselves.

The gravamen of the case against subjecting religion to the ordeal by television seems to be the danger not that religion becomes the content of television shows, but that television shows become the content of religion – the need to be televisual reshapes or distorts the Church's liturgy, preaching and even its doctrine.

Any response to these twin attacks on the need for religious broadcasting ought properly to begin by quoting Reith's dictum that the purpose of public service broadcasting is to offer everybody the best of everything. In his view, the three Charter aims of the BBC – to inform, entertain and educate – applied to every aspect of life and the totality of the human condition.

To question whether there should be music and arts programmes Reith thought philistine; to ignore sport was élitist; not to explore the sciences, luddite; to neglect news and current affairs must be to indulge in escapism. And to exclude religion was to Reith unthinkable, because for him a worthwhile programme, whatever its subject, was one that said "Yes" to life. And he believed the most resoundingly affirmative declarations about the nature of life were made by the Christian religion.

Religion is self-evidently a persistent area of experience and enquiry which no medium concerned to explore every aspect of the human condition could conceivably ignore – *persistent* because, as Jesus pointed out, if you sweep society clean of one spirit, seven more will invade the empty space. Thus, a tiny but illuminating parable: the broadcasters decided against an orthodox *Thought for the Day* spot on *Breakfast Time* and ended up with an astrologer instead.

A fair-minded observer would conclude that the society described by Bonhoeffer as maturely secular is anything but sober and down to earth; it is credulous beyond belief – zipped out on zen, mad on mantras, gone on gurus, a sucker for sufis, awed by astrology and sold on the supernatural. Religiosity is a symptom of decay in that area of experience where the supernatural invades all created life. The human response to the transcendent may be ridiculous or sublime, but it is invariable. So slam the front door on religion and it will climb back in through the window. Our so-called materialist society is not only riddled with true believers at odds about what they believe to be true, but also with exotic faiths that permeate the atmosphere seeking new churches in which to become incarnate.

So if spirituality in one form or another cannot be banished from modern society, there is no possibility of keeping it off the airwaves – from magic, mediums, exorcism, witches, telepathy at one end of the entertainment spectrum, to the pious thoughts of prominent personalities and pseudo-religious pop jingles at the other. And occupying the middle ground are radio and television adaptations of great dramas and classic stories whose themes deal with every aspect of the elemental struggle between good and evil.

The broadcasters are stuck with religion. The only question is: what sort? Here we hit a curious quirk of human nature. Most people are quite sure they know what religion is about and what makes the difference between good religion and bad, even though they will admit to being complete tyros in matters of, say, science, finance or even politics. In one sense they are right. However religion is defined, it deals in the stuff of people's ultimate concerns, and therefore their opinions about it, superficial or profound, are significant.

Yet, this amateur confidence must be qualified. The experience of faith is so subjective that those who speculate about religion without practising it are prone to a nineteenth-hole view of the vagaries of the golf course. They dredge their memories for their last regular contact with Christianity, in chapel at prep school or church parade in the army. "What was that hymn we sang at our wedding– 'tum-te-tum-te-tum divine, all human loves 'er tum-te-tum-te . . .' ".

Of all forms of human activity, none lends itself less to being treated as a spectator-sport than religion – because for much of the time there is nothing to see; the miracle of Divine love's re-creating work is happening in the secret places of the human heart, deep, deep beyond the range of the camera's eye. As Jesus said, the Kingdom of Heaven is like a seed planted deep within the ground, pushing its way imperceptibly upwards towards the light. And only the eye of faith can chart its progress.

The other necessary qualification is that Christianity is not just a spontaneous expression of the spirit, like a great fireworks display; it also burns with a steady flame which needs constant attention. Religion is a discipline which must be learned. At its heart is a simple story with a complex history whose ramifications must be painstakingly followed through. And that narrative is set out in documents written in alien languages whose original sense has to be laid bare.

The professional study of religion, therefore, demands study, reflection and intellectual skills – none of which are substitutes for a first-hand experience of the transcendent, but are necessary to authenticate religious experience and to trace back its present-day manifestations to their source in Scripture and Christian history. And since we are talking about religious broadcasting, not one but two professional disciplines are involved – theology as the science of God and communications technology as the science of broadcasting. It isn't necessary to swallow whole Neil Postman's argument that broadcasting utterly distorts religion to concede that trying to convey religious truth across the air waves makes for huge problems.

The notion, therefore, that programme makers who are specialists in current affairs or light entertainment or sport could make the odd religious programme in their spare time doesn't bear serious scrutiny. The Annan Committee's theory that religion should be spread throughout the whole range of BBC programmes would lead to the dilution and dissipation of a coherent discipline. Like science or music or drama, religion is a highly specialized subject which requires its own working teams with indisputable authority in the field. It invariably takes a connoisseur to recognize true quality and an artist to deliver it.

Neil Postman's contention that broadcasting turns religion into entertainment – as though that settled the argument – also needs to be examined carefully; there are a number of assumptions about the nature of entertainment wrapped up in it which are at least arguable.

To entertain is to occupy the mind agreeably. Strictly defined, therefore, entertainment offers an experience that is meant to be an end in itself – it has no higher aim than to pass the time as beguilingly as possible. In fact, no experience could be as vacuous as that. When people judge an entertainment programme to have been good or bad, interesting or boring, they are exercising their critical faculty, which is presumably an educative thing to do. When they discuss with their work mates what they have seen on television the night before, entertainment is performing a social function.

Because entertainment is theoretically devoid of serious purpose, its effects are insidious – cultural values are most powerfully conveyed when they pass unremarked. Thus, it may matter less that an earnest playwright preaches left-wing sermons through his characters than that a chat show host should crack racist jokes. What a panel of football experts do to the English language on *Match of the Day* may affect grammatical usage more than a dozen Brains Trust panels using words fastidiously. It is when people listen to or watch programmes with their feet up that their guard is likely to be down.

Entertainment shapes our pictures of the world. Can we therefore argue that religion should stand aloof from this process? If cultural values are transmitted imperceptibly through entertainment programmes, what about their spiritual component? Religion offers vivid pictures of the world; it advocates and sustains a powerful value-system. Therefore, without selling the pass altogether and suggesting that religion is nothing more than entertainment, its role as entertainment should at least be examined with care.

Entertainment of whatever kind is an appeal through the senses to the soul, and is intended to have a tonic or re-creational effect. It is a cordial for drooping spirits. Using John Reith's yardstick, an entertainment programme may be assumed to have said "Yes" to life if at the end of the programme people feel better for having watched or heard it. That is not a prescription for facile optimism. A drama may lacerate by its realism, but if its lingering impact leaves no room for hope, for the sense that despite everything life still has some point, then it may be many things but it is not true entertainment. And when we talk like this, are we not getting dangerously close to the concepts and vocabulary of religion?

Religion and entertainment can only be set in direct antithesis to each other on the basis of the most superficial understanding of both. Those disposed to sneer at the meretricious nature of broadcast entertainment should ponder Reith's defence of it in a valedictory speech before leaving the BBC (and this, remember, was the man popularly portrayed as a craggy Puritan élitist):

> Wholesome entertainment contributes consistently and cumulatively to the intellectual and moral happiness of the community . . . it is an investment bringing the compound interest of happier homes, broader culture and truer citizenship.

Has religion nothing to offer to that laudable goal?

Anyway, history has in a sense decided the issue. Religion has always been one of the great sources of entertainment. It spawned dance, drama, music, architecture, rhetoric, art and mime. From time immemorial, it has brightened grim and dull lives with periodic bursts of spectacle. Through festivals such as Mardi Gras and the Feast of Fools, a religion secure in its seriousness and truth could make sport of its most sacred religious practices and lampoon its usually revered leaders. Many of the great medieval festivals and riotous ecclesiastical spectacles have now vanished as a result of the enfeeblement of Western civilization's capacity for fantasy and spiritual imagination. Possibly television, with its image-making power and return to a preliterate cultural tradition, might be the unlikely engine of a new imaginative power to which religion can make cautious appeal.

None of the foregoing is intended to shrug off the main thrust of Neil Postman's criticism – though without being xenophobic, I believe it is to some extent based on his dismal American experience, where many of the TV evangelists, who are surely the limiting case, have added Impresario to the Pauline catalogue of Apostles, Prophets and Evangelists. But a blankly negative equation between religion and entertainment offers no ground for any exploration of television's religious possibilities at all.

Religious broadcasting is also needed because it is the point at which the moral and social values that underlie the whole of public service broadcasting become explicit, and are both celebrated and yet subjected to cool analysis.

What are these values that broadcasting must obviously reflect if it is not to lose touch with the public and be unable to communicate with them? Professor Basil Mitchell of Oxford, in his Gifford lectures, *Morality: Religious and Secular*, has succinctly summarized the sectional moralities of contemporary British society. All of them are reflected in the various strands of BBC programming.

Scientific, industrial, nature and environmental programmes reflect the values of scientific humanism. It is from the unflinching facing of facts that values are discovered. If two people or groups disagree on a matter of morality, one of them must be mistaken, and even though at first we may not know which one, in the end more knowledge through research will settle the issue.

Then there is what might be called romantic humanism. Music, arts, drama, some forms of comedy and certainly most youth programmes celebrate the values which undergird the freedom, spontaneity and creativity of the individ-

145

ual. Romantics have no desire to impose their moral values on others; they seek only to answer the question: how shall I live? Different people will give different answers to that question, and one person may give different answers to it at different times without any sense of incongruity.

Sincerity and commitment are the cardinal virtues of romantic humanism, and the artist – whether writer, painter or pop star – is the cultural hero or heroine. The era of the Flower People, of the permissive society, of *Honest to God*, of student protest, of the Swinging Sixties were the peaks of romantic humanism, though the spirit still haunts the imagination of many ageing hippies who react sharply against the ethos of Thatcherism and the yuppy culture of the City institutions.

Possibly the dominant sectional morality as reflected in BBC programmes is that of liberal humanism. Tolerance, freedom of expression, fairness and impartiality are the values which have characterized the approach to most areas of factual programmes, especially news and current affairs. Indeed, the BBC as an institution is a concrete endorsement of the values of liberal democracy. In 1968 the BBC published a pamphlet called *Broadcasting and the Public Mood* which declared that the Corporation had no intention of remaining neutral about moral values. "We know", it said, "that hatred, cruelty and intolerance are bad, and that love, kindness and truthfulness are good."

A somewhat vapid version of this liberalism even permeates light entertainment programmes such as soap operas. Good more or less triumphs over evil, everything just about works out right in the end, people other than stereotype villains tend to do the decent thing, and in the spectrum of mood which ranges from optimism to despair, the needle always settles a little shakily in the sunny sector, come the last act. This whole ethos may be too material-istic for those of austere taste, but there is no vicious ideology underlying the narrative likely to brutalize the viewer.

Meanwhile, a sizeable core of people within society still consider themselves bound by a system of values which derives its sanctions from some form of religious belief, predominantly Christianity, Judaism and Islam. They believe not in co-existing moralities but in a moral law which is binding on all, even those who turn their backs on it. In an age of moral relativities, these believers insist that there are bedrock certainties to which appeal can be made.

It is a revised and relaxed version of this value system that underlies religious broadcasting, and which it brings to bear critically upon other sectional moralities, especially in its documentary programmes. For the first question religious broadcasting is concerned to answer in its factual programmes is: what is faith doing in the world? And the answer might range from celebrating to suffering by way of all the dilemmas, emotions and reactions faith evokes. The second question runs: what does the contemporary world look like through the eyes of faith? It is this second strand of programmes that looks at values, seeking the truth behind the facts, offering a distinctive perspective on subjects that may have been dealt with in other areas of output such as news and current affairs or science.

In this, the religious department is doing precisely what the Annan Committee described as the distinctive work of religion – "reminding the moralists of spiritual values and the social scientists of the inevitability of moral choice". But with this difference: Annan left the question of worship in mid-air, whereas religious broadcasting regards worship as the lynch-pin of its output. For worship is about people addressing the transcendent directly. In so doing, it testifies to the fact that the rationale for the religious department's existence is not illusory, and thus validates the rest of its programmes. Christian values can only be brought to bear upon issues of the day provided the source of those values is regularly and publicly acknowledged. So unless other departments are prepared to make worship a central part of their output – and not even the most imperialistic of other programme bosses has shown any interest in annexing this territory – they cannot discharge religious broadcasting's other functions.

Finally, the question of whether religious broadcasting is needed has already been decided pragmatically by the growth of religious departments in most public service broadcasting organizations. They have expanded not by bureaucratic inflation but by the influx of young programme makers who find religion a challenging, baffling and exhilarating area of human experience on which to bring to bear faith or scepticism in varying proportions. The days have long gone when religious broadcasting was the preserve of superannuated parsons with a yen for amateur dramatics or elocutory gifts nourished in cathedral choir stalls.

One reason why highly accomplished young broadcasting professionals are drawn to religion has to do with the nature of the medium as a form of communication. Unlike preaching, teaching or public oratory, in broadcasting, neither party – communicators or those being communicated with – usually knows who the other party is. The public's interests, tastes and dislikes can only be guessed at or assessed by rough and ready survey methods. Therefore programme makers dare not aim for the periphery of the target for fear of missing it altogether and committing an act of non-communication. They must go for the bull – the heart of the culture where most people congregate, their lives governed by simple ideas, broad emotional experiences, predictable tastes and home-spun convictions.

The fancy way of putting this is to say that all forms of mass communication must aim at the central meaning systems of a society – whose identity is given shape by the power of the available imaginative materials contained in stories, models, symbols and moving images. And historically, because Western secular society has been decisively shaped by the Christian religion, its concepts, vocabulary and traditions form one of those central meaning systems. Therefore, to some of those who are stimulated by the intellectual challenges of mass communication, religious broadcasting is intriguing.

In however distorted or even bizarre a form, the spectre of God still haunts the collective memory of our society. There is something there for the broadcaster to home in on with some hope of touching a nerve. In this sense, religion, far from being a peripheral and rather esoteric subject, belongs properly to main-stream broadcasting.

Is it Committed Enough?

The arrival on British TV screens of the U.S. television evangelists in programmes bursting with colour, excitement and, above all, spiritual fervour, has led some British Christians to bewail the laid-back, cool and doctrinally diffuse style of BBC and ITV religion. Why, they complain, does *Morning Worship* have to be so wishy-washy, the *Daily Service* so middle-class, and *Thought for the Day* so secular? Why can't we hear preachers who believe

passionately in Bible-based religion, who aren't so accom-
modating of secular culture that they'd add the Devil to
the Trinity in the interests of ecumenicity?

This criticism has been somewhat muted by the sexual
and financial scandals which have undermined the reputation of some TV evangelists. But there is a serious point
here, which is not fully met by pointing out that comparing
British public service religious broadcasting unfavourably
with U.S. television evangelism is like castigating a stained
glass window for not being a magnifying glass. The
window must collect and diffuse the whole light spectrum
across the wide area, whereas the magnifying glass concen-
trates burning rays on one tiny spot.

The character of religious broadcasting in Britain has
been moulded by three main kinds of forces – historical,
to do with the way the BBC developed; structural, because
of the properties of broadcasting as a medium; and theological, reflected in changes in British society's religious
profile and the traditions evolved by successive generations
of religious broadcasters.

The giant shadow of John Reith, the BBC's founding
father, still looms today over British religious broadcasting. He was a pioneer ecumenist who believed denomi-
nationalism was a hindrance to the spread of the Christian
faith, and that broadcasting waves could overleap the
walls of sectarianism by appealing directly to people in
their homes. From the moment he joined the infant BBC
in 1922 he declared that broadcast worship was important
but that it should be "unassociated with any particular
creed or denomination". He appointed a group of clergy
to plan religious broadcasts, and made sure it contained
a Roman Catholic priest and a Free Church minister.

When Canon Dick Sheppard agreed to conduct the first

experimental broadcast service from St Martin in the Fields in January 1924, Reith laid down only one condition: the liturgy must be "interdenominational". Where else in the world other than on BBC radio were regular interdenominational services held as a matter of course in the early 1920s?

It was Reith's passionate conviction that radio could be a powerful agency of evangelism. When the Dean and Chapter of St Paul's refused to allow a live transmission of Evensong from the Cathedral in 1926, because they feared it might deplete Sunday congregations throughout the land, Reith retorted, "Even if this were so, it is probably of small moment compared to the numbers who are now hearing what they would otherwise not hear. If the churches recognize their new opportunity, there will not be room enough to hold their people."

Reith, unlike most of the TV evangelists, saw religious broadcasting as an adjunct to the work of the churches, not an attempt to supersede it. The aim was to whet the appetite of non-believers and to offer aid and comfort to Christians unable to get along to their local churches. For years, the opening announcement of the weekly Evensong from Westminster Abbey included the phrase, "For the special benefit of the sick".

So, from the outset, Reith turned his back on the magnifying glass approach to religion – the choice of one denomination or theological position as the official religious stance of the BBC. He consciously shaped religious broadcasting as a force for ecumenical co-operation in British life. And he chose as staff and contributors to religious programmes only those who shared his abhorrence of sectarianism and denominational spikiness. The bigot and hard-line dogmatist got short shrift on the air-waves when Reith ran the BBC.

The other factor which decided fatefully the BBC's approach to religious broadcasting derived not from Reith's veneration of God but his attitude to Mammon. Believing the BBC was a national asset, he argued for and got a system of financing based on a licence fee. The licence fee was the symbol of a covenant relationship between the British people and the BBC, whereby the Corporation undertook to provide them with broadcasting that reflected the best of everything that was being said, thought and done, in return for financial security.

Because the licence fee was a tax rather than a voluntary contribution, it meant that everyone who held one had a reasonable entitlement to have his or her general interests reflected on the airwaves. Thus, in general programmes, the BBC was committed to *broad*casting as opposed to *narrow*casting; and in religion, it undertook to reflect the breadth and richness of the religious life of Britain. The Wee Free licence fee payer in the Outer Hebrides had as much right to expect his religious convictions to be heard over the wireless as had the Anglican licence fee payer in the South East. The BBC was locked into electronic ecumenicity as much by legal contract as by John Reith's evangelical zeal.

In the 1920s and 1930s, offering a broadly comprehensive religious programme service presented no insuperable difficulties. Reith, who had a real gift for finding simple solutions to complex problems, came up with his "Four Sundays" policy. Each month, two Sundays were given over to the Anglicans, one to the Roman Catholics and one to the Free Churches. Should there be a fifth Sunday in the month, Reith offered it to either the Salvation Army or the Quakers, two bodies of which he warmly approved.

None of Reith's successors has been so lucky in having to hand such a sublimely simple formula. The Four Sundays policy no longer corresponds to statistical reality. The present religious diversity of British society means that in addition to many Christian denominations, ranging from the main-stream to the exotic, there are sizeable communities of devout Muslim, Hindu, Jewish and Sikh licence fee payers who expect their religious convictions to be taken account of on the air-waves.

So present-day religious broadcasters face the challenge of trying to reflect the whole spectrum of religious experience without turning the air-waves into a sort of electronic Babel. They are bound to fail, but because they have been tutored in the ecumenical spirit of Reith, they try to see that no significant religious movement or position goes unremarked.

The alternative is the U.S. policy which permits the richest believers to buy most time on television and radio. With all its weaknesses, British religious broadcasting does not allow Mammon to determine which of God's spokesmen has the loudest voice and the longest exposure on the air-waves. Reith's licence fee may have confronted religious broadcasters with an impossible problem in trying to satisfy the multifarious spiritual expectations of thirty million customers, but at least it is a bulwark against cheque-book religion.

This built-in electronic ecumenism may seem to protect religious broadcasters from having to stand up and be counted on behalf of one dogmatic position rather than another; in fact, it taxes their religious integrity to the limit. For they are not doctrinal eunuchs. They have their own cherished beliefs which they must sublimate in order to provide a platform for the effective expression of religious convictions they may disagree with or even find abhorrent.

The good religious programme makers need more than mere tolerance – they need the liberal spirit which agrees that all voices should be heard in the market place of ideas. It takes a special kind of charity to ensure that religious opinions a producer finds uncongenial or even erroneous are projected as convincingly as the medium will allow. Good religious broadcasters are those whose theology can find room for Voltaire's dictum, "I disagree with what you say, but I'll fight to the death for your right to say it". And the tradition is passed on from generation to generation.

Most people known to me who work in religious broadcasting have a healthy horror of creating by default precisely that state of affairs television evangelists strive assiduously to achieve – a substitute church which has no existence outside the air-waves, and whose members have no responsibilities other than pressing a switch and staying awake in their armchairs. This salutary diffidence produces over time a mind-set not hospitable to rigorously dogmatic expressions of religion which might be magnified by the distorting prism of the medium, thus giving high definition to some manifestation of the ghostly Church of the Air that hovers around.

The truth is that dogmatic religion divides; and that's fine, but not on the air-waves. It is the stuff on which inquisitions flourish, and of which martyrdoms are made. All honour to those prepared to die for the minutiae of doctrine, but broadcasting is a medium of consensus, not of division. Its tendency is to create social cohesion rather than nonconformity.

The religious broadcaster must choose subjects and styles of treatment likely to embrace the largest possible number of viewers and listeners. This, of course, opens the broadcaster to the charge expressed in the Gospel parody of being one of the bland leading the bland into every ditch in sight. And yet this desire to reach the general public without provoking division is an honourable aim the religious broadcaster shares with the evangelist. The evangelist sticks to a Gospel pared down to essentials – the great sweeping affirmations of faith. Doctrinal nitpicking may come later.

One of the counts against some, though not all, of the U.S. television preachers, is precisely that they lack the generosity of spirit demonstrated by the great evangelists and are dogmatists of the harshest type. They publicly castigate their enemies, chief amongst whom are communists, homosexuals, secular humanists, pacifists, schools that teach evolution, judges opposed to capital punishment, liberal theologians, the World Council of Churches and Roman Catholicism. It could be argued that the TV evangelists pay through the nose for the privilege of indulging their sectarianism. But it is unthinkable that the British public, through the licence fee, would underwrite religious broadcasting shot through with barely concealed hatreds and dissensions likely to add to the tensions of an already polarized society.

Certainly, in seeking to achieve broad appeal, mainstream British religious broadcasting is always in danger of leaching out the tougher doctrinal content from its programmes and offering the public a milk and water diet rather than the strong meat of faith. But some of the exasperation of British Christians at this state of affairs is based on false expectations of what religious broadcasting can do. Neither constitutionally nor theologically has religious broadcasting a mandate to do the Church's job for it.

On the "he who pays the piper" principle, U.S. religious programmes are openly propagandist on behalf of the churches, individuals or organizations who pay for the air time. But it is the British public who are the paymasters of public service religious broadcasting, and a long time ago they decreed through Parliament that the BBC should be debarred from engaging in propaganda of however high-minded a kind. That ban applies right across the board, as much to religion as to any other area of output.

The price of religious broadcasting forswearing any denominational or doctrinal allegiance is the forfeiture of the passionate advocacy of a single viewpoint, the burning intensity of dogmatic certitude; the bonus is the freedom to subject to cool examination every aspect of religion on behalf of a public at once sceptical of its claims and yet intrigued by them.

This measured, unhysterical approach to religious broadcasting is likely to come into its own as the Television Age wears on and, by courtesy of satellite, the whole world is transformed into one gigantic television audience. Ecumenicity is about to take on a whole new meaning, as from every point on the globe a plethora of religious events, experiences and personalities press in on the individual television viewer. A veritable Babel of ghostly voices will canvass the claims of this or that dogmatism.

Increasingly, public service religious broadcasting, because of its financial and ecclesiastical independence and its tradition of occupying the middle ground, will find itself fulfilling that Pauline role of testing the spirits to see whether they be of God. And though the devotees of high-octane religion will tune in to the station of their choice, the bemused enquirer reeling from the sales pitch of highly competitive religious propagandists may find in mainstream religious broadcasting some kind of benchmark by which to measure the rest.

It was G. K. Chesterton who in his *Introduction to the Book of Job* wrote, "A man can no more possess a private religion than he can possess a private sun and moon." In a multiverse of private religions, mainstream religious broadcasting, for all its infuriating even-handedness and intellectualism, represents public religion. Its concern is to inform, educate and entertain the human spirit. The rest is up to the real-life communities of faith – churches, temples, synagogues and mosques.

NINE

THE AWFUL TEMPTATIONS OF HUMBERT CULPEPPER

It is a well-attested fact that those who handle sacred things are subject to special temptations. Far from close proximity to the Holy of Holies conferring a special exemption from sin upon us, we are in most peril just when we think we are safest. Not for nothing is the Devil in the proverb referred to as the ape of god. Falsehood is never so false as when it is very nearly true. Anti-Christ appears before us not sporting horns and a tail but looking for all the world as though he had just stepped down out of a stained glass window, complete with the crown of Heaven upon his head – though he wears it slightly askew, which gives the game away.

This is a glum reflection on the special temptations assailing the religious broadcaster. The power and privilege of addressing the Gospel to millions of people at the same time, right there in their own homes, are obvious. But what about the obverse side of the coin? It is a biblical insight that power always exacts too high a price for its services. We cannot handle even the holiest of levers without getting our fingers bruised occasionally.

I could go on at boring length about the virtues of religious programme makers I have known, but here I want to consider their special temptations, their besetting sins. I shall attempt to do this, not from any position of cool objectivity, like someone studying the inmates of an aquarium from outside the tank. I'm right there in the water with them. It was John Ruskin who noted tersely in his diary, "Heard an excellent sermon. Applied it to myself". That's what I intend to do.

And I shall approach the task by way of parody. As scientists put it in their awful jargon, this will be a "worst case scenario". I have conjured out of thin air a strictly fictitious religious producer who rejoices in the name of Humbert Culpepper. Knowing my luck, there is probably someone in the broadcasting business with that precise name already beating a path to the door of the nearest libel lawyer. So let me hasten to declare that Humbert is a travesty. He is not *exactly* like me nor remotely like anyone else I've ever met in broadcasting. What follows could be called a work of admonitory fiction.

We broadcasters are an arrogant breed. Here is Humbert, twenty-odd years old, with the bloom of the Bible school still upon his cheeks, complete with a BBC identity card and the mandatory stop watch, tutting and shaking his head. He is staring severely at the script humbly offered him by an eminent professor of theology, who is flattered beyond belief that he has been asked to address the public over the air-waves for five minutes about a subject on which he is a world authority.

In a breath-taking reversal of roles, the novice marks the expert's paper. "Won't do, you know", says Humbert, glumly, pointing accusingly at this phrase or that. "Radio Four listeners won't buy that." Head bowed, aghast at his gaucherie, the professor obediently scores out the offending words. How could he have lived so long, met so many people, wrestled so passionately to express the precise truth about an imprecise Reality using the crude tool of language, and yet still know so little about communication?

In fairness to Humbert, like God, he is no respecter of persons. The scripts of professors of theology and bus conductors alike are blasted by his searing eye. Indeed, were a small town carpenter from Nazareth called Joshua to pitch up with a script, titled with stunning unoriginality "The Beatitudes", Humbert would decree that *nine* beatitudes is a couple too many. Too dense, too repetitive. And the rest could do with some "unpacking" — to use Humbert's favourite word. Four or at most five would make a nice, tight script. Moses wouldn't fare much better. Humbert's feeling is that the title "Ten Commandments" should be changed to "Ten Suggestions", on the grounds that the public hates being told what to do.

The point is that Humbert is an authority on something called mass communication. He is privy to the wishes and tastes of an unseen, unknown body of viewers and listeners whose appetites are so unpredictable that broadcasting organizations spend a fortune on audience research, and still end up squandering millions of pounds on programmes nobody wants to watch or listen to. Even the mandarins of broadcasting don't *know* what the public wants, though they don't know for more sophisticated reasons than the rest of us.

Humbert *knows* what the religious constituency wants. And he knows, not because he is a close friend or even a nodding acquaintance of G. K. Chesterton's "man on the Clapham omnibus", but because he talks regularly to his fellow producers down the corridor and respects their programme judgement. And they *know* because they know

Humbert and other producers who know – and so on ad infinitum in ever decreasing magic circles.

In truth, Humbert in his concrete and glass tower is probably more isolated from the public than most professors of theology will ever be. For he is a Media Person. He rubs shoulders with the stars. Nay, why cavil? He employs them. With a power unequalled since the days of the Papal Banned Books Index, Humbert decides who and what the public will hear and see. He moves, enveloped in a golden glow, through a world ordinary people only catch a glimpse of as they are conducted round the gleaming temples of Media Magic. "Thought I might ask Terry to present *Songs of Praise* occasionally", he muses aloud at the bar of the local, to the wonder of everyone within earshot. Who can blame Humbert for claiming as his due the public's envious estimate of him? He has started to believe his own mythology.

Closely allied to Humbert's arrogance is his talent for mystification. He can bamboozle the most intelligent outsider with torrents of jargon about processes and machinery so rarified as to make Sanskrit sound like a universal language. Were this same outsider to observe Humbert at work, it would slowly dawn on him that Humbert's much-vaunted mastery of media mystery is actually a certain judgement and facility acquired by doing the same thing over and over again. It is a perfectly decent, indeed, essential skill, but one more akin to that of a cook throwing a perfect pancake than of Einstein evolving the special theory of relativitiy.

The public doesn't want to believe that, of course. It prefers to cling to the illusion that Humbert is a magician. If he were to behave like a contemporary freemason, throw open the lodge doors and reveal his modest secrets, there would be rioting in the streets. To this extent, Humbert is more the victim of a mystique than its perpetrator. The public requires broadcasters to be masters and mistresses of complex skills. For if broadcasting is a modest craft, then programmes are just crude entertainment and not high art. And this makes the public seem weak-willed rather than highly discriminating in allowing themselves to be chained to the television set or radio for hours every day.

Truth to tell, Humbert himself is susceptible to the media mystification virus because deep down he is in awe of the power he commands. Here he is, resplendent with an Oxbridge degree in Classics or even an A-level in Media Studies, as a producer-director, commanding an army of technicians, a studio the size of the main concourse at Heathrow Airport, and millions of pounds of gleaming equipment: at least, for a couple of hours at a time. Not for him the hundreds of hours of lonely vigil in the sky that an airline pilot must endure before being allowed to control technology of a comparable cost and sophistication.

If Humbert's chosen medium is radio rather than television, the nature of the mystique is radically different but almost as potent. In television, he is a general leading an army into battle; in radio he is the lone prophet addressing the people from the mountain top, or more accurately, supporting the arms of the one who is doing the talking. If the visitor off the street is dazzled by the organizing power of the television producer as team leader, he is equally awed by the solitary eminence of the radio producer who, single-handedly, can mediate his words to the millions. The tumult of the television studio and the eerie silence of the radio studio speak of media power with equal eloquence.

If arrogance and mystification are two of Humbert's besetting sins, snobbery is a third. As a parish curate, Humbert would probably have to wait a fortnight for an interview with his diocesan bishop, but armed with his Uher tape recorder and uttering the magic incantation "BBC!" he strolls through the gilded portals barred to all but the Mighty, the Great and the Good. Cardinals, Moderators, Chief Rabbis, pop stars and Cabinet ministers fall like chaff before the winnower's scythe.

The usually inaccessible moguls of modern life clear their crowded diaries to meet Humbert's remorseless production schedules. "Call me Mike", says the Archbishop, offering the most comfortable chair in his study and his best sherry to a blasé Humbert, who hums and haws and discusses dates and times. He refuses the sherry because he is in a hurry. His next port of call is Buckingham Palace, where a Very Important Personage is doing a *Thought for the Day* if Humbert likes the script.

There are many reasons why even the greatest and most powerful in the land wish to impose their opinions, convictions and prejudices on the public. For some, it is a simple matter of finding the most powerful megaphone available through which to publish some credo they wish to share with others. Then there are those for whom the electronic media offer a variant of Descartes' dictum, "I think, therefore I am" – "I have appeared on television, therefore I am important".

Radio and television are the great validating agencies of our time, offering fame, wealth and significance of an ephemeral sort to those who can gain access to them. And there at the barrier is Humbert with his rubber stamp, marking the passports of aspirants, separating out the sheep to whom the medium will offer fleeting immortality from the goats who are banished into the outer darkness of obscurity.

The electronic media short-circuit the customary class and status barriers, bringing people like Humbert into intimate contact with those who would otherwise be impregnable in their unapproachability. The problem is that if Humbert is not ruthlessly frank in his self-appraisal, he may begin to believe that he is being sought after and fêted for his wit, intelligence and sheer lovableness.

But Humbert is not just the confidant and friend of the mighty; he may indeed be their saviour. "My God!" he confides to his colleagues along the corridor. "The bishop made a hash of that interview. Luckily, I can edit out the fluffs. It should work." "Work" — there's that magic media-verb popping up again. Not "Is it true, honest and of good report?" but "Will it work?"

And when the good bishop hears himself the next morning on the radio, he is quietly pleased at his fluency and polish. His disembodied voice has been purged of every hesitation and repetition. He enjoys the illusion of perfection. For Humbert is a closet-gnostic, an unconscious devotee of the oldest Christian heresy. He wants to spiritualize away all evidence of raw flesh and blood imperfections in his contributors as he edits out errors and produces an impression of unearthly faultlessness. Plotinus would have been proud of him.

Humbert's delight in mixing with the mighty would be a harmless conceit except that it can distort his professional judgement by providing him with a self-selecting élite to whose opinions he gives undue weight because he enjoys ease of access to them. "I'll give the Moderator a ring and get him into the studio for a comment", he says casually. It could well be that some unknown inner-city curate might be much better informed on the issue in question, but he isn't a Name. For even in the hallowed world of religion there are prominent personalities of whom it could justly be said that their name is worth more than their services.

There is not infrequently a dramatic contrast between the titles and trappings of celebrity and the modest reality within. Humbert is so taken with the ornateness of the parcel's wrapping that he ignores the plainness of the contents. To be famous for being well-known is the standard definition of media celebrity, and Humbert must work within such lunatic parameters.

Most of the foregoing parodies the besetting sins of all broadcasters and not simply those whose theme is religion. But there are other temptations, or at least inevitable theological distortions, which Humbert shares with every religious broadcaster, however gifted or experienced. For instance, there is that business of reversing the Incarnation.

Christianity robustly declares that the Word became flesh. Humbert and his colleagues are busy turning flesh back into words. They take human beings, put them in front of a camera or a microphone, and transform them into disembodied words or ghostly images. The act of broadcasting, however well-intentioned, tears apart the unity of word and action personified in and by Jesus. The gospel message is always incarnate in the person of the messenger so that the hearers can judge the worth of both together, asking in effect, "Can I trust this one? Are his words and his actions all of a piece?"

The essence of true communication is self-disclosure, but such personal unveiling as the broadcaster achieves is structured, formal and as little revelatory as a signature at the foot of a newspaper editorial; it invites relationship with a cipher. And, of course, I as a hearer or viewer cannot make any free response to the person addressing me through the television screen or radio receiver. I may react to the broadcaster's words, be beguiled or irritated by a tone of voice or an expression in the eyes, but nothing I say or do will stem the flow of eloquence or modify the structure of a single sentence. Even as the ghost addresses me, I could cut my throat, lie down in front of the television screen and die, and the rhetoric would still surge on remorselessly.

Since the absolute distinction between Old and New Testaments is the enfleshment of the message, it could be argued that religious broadcasting, for all its technical sophistication, belongs to the old dispensation rather than the new.

Humbert himself might claim that it is a Stonehenge view of science, theology or liturgy, to insist that mere physical contact is always more authentic than spiritual communion. May not a broadcast act of worship heard over a car radio on a motorway be a more intimate experience than rubbing shoulders with strangers in church, or, more likely, in a sparsely attended modern church, sharing a physical space the size of a football pitch with a few dozen widely scattered fellow-worshippers? And what about the Communion of Saints? Surely no Christian doubts that we may commune intimately with them even though we are denied physical contact?

Fair point. But it is not for choice that fellowship within the Communion of Saints is strictly physical rather than corporeal. The operation of biological laws inhibits what all Christians would surely prefer — the full sensuous

166

experience of love, even at the price of vulnerability and openness. It's the old gnostic pit yawning under our feet again. Those who *for choice* prefer spiritual communion with other believers to corporeal presence may end up settling for a substitute Church of the Air which has no existence outside the ether, whose members have no responsibilities beyond pressing a switch and staying awake.

Ths historical community of faith makes, in Christ's name, ultimate demands in loving and being loved, forgiving and being forgiven. And this surely means that we be *there* to bleed if necessary for our professions of faith, hope and love. So Humbert and his colleagues stub their toes against the Incarnation – and, as we all do, against the Cross, that symbol of God's impotence prevailing over earthly might. For in the league table of secular power structures, the electronic media must rank high amongst the most pervasive and potent. Christian broadcasters, therefore, in trying to proclaim the Gospel of the Cross from positions of immense secular power, are like the millionaire preaching the virtues of poverty from the back seat of a gold-plated Rolls Royce.

These media power concentrations are under the sketchiest of public control. They do not pretend to be democratic; ordinary people have virtually no access to them except in token ways; they are the embodiment of just those social, economic and cultural forces against which Jesus expressed his harshest anathemas.

Humbert *is* a parody. His real-life counterparts are acutely aware of the theological contradictions in what they are trying to do, and never cease to ask fundamental questions about their work. They are not seduced by the aura of glamour that attaches to the electronic media, especially television because of its immediacy, drama and vivid impact. There is truly spiritual harrowing in their strange vocation.

Yet they also know that they have got to go on attempting the impossible because it is only through the television screen or radio loudspeaker that millions will hear anything that sounds remotely like the Gospel. This means that Humbert Culpepper and all who follow his trade are playing for rather large stakes. And in his moments of candour, Humbert consoles himself with the knowledge that, after all, God did once speak through the jawbone of an ass, so there's still hope for him.

TEN

HARK! THE HERALD ANGEL RINGS!

Herewith some thoughts about the religious significance of the electronic media themselves.

According to one biblical reference book, "Angels are messengers; their nature is of no consequence."[14] They are spirit without flesh, capable of instant transportation and existing only to serve the message they bring. The popular idea that they are disembodied bundles of virtue, beings of supernatural purity, is wide of the mark. Job says that God finds fault with angels, and Jesus declared that the date of the end of the world is kept secret from them. Indeed, in the Old Testament all manner of impersonal agents ranging from the wind to the plague do service as angels.

In the modern world, the angelic medium is electricity. It is impersonal, instantaneous, and universal, having no intrinsic significance except to transmit messages. And like the Almighty dispatching his messengers from a celestial control point beyond the stars to the furthest reaches of the universe, so electricity operates from the centre to the margins – power station to the national grid; telephone exchange to millions of phone sockets.

As a communications medium, electricity has transformed both our personal lives and the power-structures of our society. Take just one embodiment of the angelic medium, the telephone. From the early days when the invention gave birth to an adjective "phoney", meaning bogus, unreal, having no more substance than a chat with a ghost, the telephone has become a dominant and dominating form of human discourse.

It is imperious. Friends interrupt intimate conversations when the phone rings; people passing a public phone box will stop and answer a call that could not possibly be for them. Marshall McLuhan repeats a *New York Times* account of Howard Unruh, a mad sniper, who in 1949 killed thirteen people and then barricaded himself in his house for a shoot-out to the death with the police. An enterprising reporter discovered the phone number of the house. The killer stopped shooting, put down his rifle and answered the phone. "What is it?", he asked. "I can't talk now, I'm busy."

The telephone is not a general disseminator of information, it demands a personal partner. It assumes total and instant availability. To leave one's telephone off the cradle is the ultimate anti-social gesture. It is as though one were opting out of the human race. Indeed, if we must move outside the range of our telephone we usually employ an answering service or a recording machine to ensure that we have missed nothing.

Most people even regard the telephone's nuisance potential as a virtue. There is an old music hall joke about the woman who was so lonely she took three baths in quick succession in the hope the telephone would ring. It is the only device of modern civilization whose capacity to cause inconvenience is one of its attractions. The ringing phone promises an unexpected new twist in the usually predictable course of our lives. It is no coincidence that in a modern play the dramatic device which signals a sudden development of the plot is often the telephone — "At that moment, the phone rang".

Primitive peoples separate spirit from flesh only in their dreams, myths and rituals. Throughout their ordinary lives, the spirit is locked up inside their flesh. The telephone enables the Westerner to remain anchored to the spot and travel in spirit — with interesting effects on his or her psyche. Psychiatrists report that patients who are grossly neurotic often behave perfectly normally with a phone in their hands. And there are people with severe speech impairments who never fluff a syllable over the telephone. Their spirits seem to be liberated from the constraints of maimed personalities.

On the other hand, some people of the mildest disposition are provoked to brusqueness and even hostility by the disembodied voice at the other end of the line. It is as though the ancient fear of the unknown outsider as a presumed enemy still forces its way up through the collective unconscious. Because they can't look into the eyes of the person to whom they are speaking, or observe the position of his sword hand, they feel vaguely threatened.

To insist that one's phone number is not commonly available to whoever cares to consult a telephone directory — to be "ex-directory" — is the nearest one can get in a democratic society to that hierarchy of human discourse whereby subjects must not take the initiative and address the Monarch unless she speaks first. The privileged are immune from the claims made against them by the generality. They can speak when they choose but do not have to listen. And by the same inversion of privilege, they can choose not to give us their exclusive attention. Whoever pitches up to meet us bearing in his hand a portable telephone is open to other claims on his concentration.

171

Because sound, unlike sight, has no focal point or location — we talk of a night "being filled with music" — it is the true ecumenical medium; it hooks us into a universal community. We are only as far from it as the nearest socket. Not to be reachable, unless by deliberate choice, is to be of little account. Indeed, the degree of personal access to a telephone is an index of power. The poor must queue at a public call box: then there is an ascending scale — a telephone in the house, a receiver in every room, a phone in the car, and finally one which will fit into a brief-case.

It was Marshall McLuhan who spelt out the extent to which electricity in the form of telephone and telegraph has changed the power-structures of the world. Because the centre can be in touch with the margins instantly, the old devolved patterns of power have been by-passed. There was a time when diplomacy was an advanced skill because the ambassador or plenipotentiary in foreign parts, in the absence of instructions from his masters, had the full responsibility of caring for his country's interests. Until the next diplomatic bag arrived after a laborious journey via coach, ship and despatch rider, he was the executive arm of his government; his decision committed his nation.

Now it has all changed. When crisis looms, the President in the White House picks up the hot-line telephone and speaks directly to the General Secretary in the Kremlin. So all intermediate levels of responsibility are down-graded. The carefully structured pyramids of power as forms of executive control evolved over centuries can be short-circuited by a single telephone call.

Edmund Carpenter[15] describes how when Lester Pearson took over as Prime Minister of Canada he mislaid the hot-line telephone somewhere amidst the clutter of his huge office. One day in 1964 it rang, and he couldn't find it.

"My God," said the minister who was with him, "do you realize this could mean war?"

"No," Pearson replied, "they can't start a war if we don't answer it."

This is a new and alarming concept of power based on the telephone as the agent of instant decision. In the era of the document, there was time to ponder, to have second thoughts, to pause as the pen traversed the paper, even to screw it up and start again. Now the survival of the planet might depend on the instant reaction of an over-tired President responding to a curt question from an old enemy over a crackling line.

All the foregoing prompts the thought that whereas even the commercial college teaches trainee secretaries how to use the telephone without any fancy philosophizing about it, the place where the fancy philosophizing ought to take place – the theological seminary – seems totally oblivious of its significance. The godly professors will wrestle in biblical exegesis with the significance of "fallen" angels, or why they left their "former estate", or whether the "angel of his presence" refers to the Messiah or to Gabriel, or why manna is "angel food", or how angels bear the souls of the redeemed to paradise. For these are likely examination subjects. But which theological faculty ever set questions about the theology of the telephone?

Then the professor is called out of the room. Telephone. An angel demands his presence – one that will decisively affect the lives of his students and of the world within which they will minister. But it will go theologically unremarked. As the Epistle to the Hebrews points out, sometimes we "entertain an angel unawares".

Exercising Religious Muscles

Human beings are inveterately religious. Even atheists admit as much, though they regard it as an unfortunate hang-over from a previous stage of human development which we will some day outgrow. Karl Marx was no lover of religion, but he did not underestimate its power. He was often misunderstood when he declared that religion is the opium of the people. He wasn't talking about escapism but strong comfort, for as the rest of the quotation runs, "Religion is the sigh of the oppressed creature, just as it is the spirit of a spiritless situation."

Religion persists because we cannot know everything about literally anything and will always hope that what is beyond our knowledge is better than anything we do know. It is in the discrepancy, that perceptual crevice between what is and our sense of what ought be, that religion breeds. At the fuzzy boundary between the natural and the supernatural we may dimly apprehend the presence of a reality distinct from and beyond the world. We may address it as He, She or It, but the moment we say "You" we are in at the deep end.

This is not to concede the simple evangelical assertion that our society always teeters on the brink of religious revival and needs only a charismatic reincarnation of Luther, Wesley, or Moody, powered by the prayers of a faithful remnant, to drive people back to the pews in droves. Equally, it is not to dispute that revivals do occur; they are outworkings of that Spirit which blows where it chooses, and are acts of grace to be received with gratitude. But in Western society, many decades of secularity cover the religious impulse of the general population, and it is unlikely this shell will be blasted away in one great volcanic spiritual eruption.

But even in a secular society, certain archetypal themes run through the life and experience of believers and unbelievers alike. Their lives are touched by dread and glory, unearthly fears have to be subdued and some sort of response made to the ultimate questions of life and death. People still need to locate themselves in the universe, in society and in their own heads.

The human spirit-life does not wither because official religion is enfeebled. It still feeds on the raw material of religious experience wherever it may be found. And television is one such source which offers a store of stories, images, models and symbols to keep in trim what could be called the human religious muscles – awaiting a higher manifestation of the Spirit on which they might be exercised.

Take people's deep need for ritual. Ritual is the ceremonial re-enactment of the stories by which we live. By imposing order on an untidy, frightening and unpredictable world, ritual directs human beings into the flow of sacred power in the way iron filings line up in response to magnetic influence. Ritual takes place in a sacred space, set apart from the routine spaces of ordinary life. Sacred space may be contained within an elaborate architectual edifice like a cathedral, or on bare ground marked by the graves of gods and ancestors as in African tribal religion. The space is specially ordered to make communion possible.

Ritual time is also sacred. It is not measured by the clock but forms a carefully structured unity which encompasses a beginning, a middle and an end. In ordinary life we are always in the middle of the "now" — a time-flow whose beginnings have slipped far behind us and whose climax is surrounded in uncertainty. In ritual time we are not frozen in the present but can project ourselves both forwards and backwards to contemplate our origins and destiny.

The core of all ritual is the story of a crucial event considered so important that it generates loyalty in all who hear it. Whether the event is real or legendary, in the act of recalling it, its original power is released. The participant in ritual withdraws from the world into a special space, time and action, in order to return to everyday life with renewed strength and confidence.

Television is a ritual medium in the sense that it operates in a special space. The screen is a window opening on to a world which has its own private existence and yet entices viewers to enter because it mirrors the world with which they are familiar. And television-time is a special time. Satellites have abolished time-zones so that today and tomorrow coalesce in the urgent Now of a television programme which can be seen simultaneously from one end of the world to the other. And on earth, the town and the country, which have traditionally observed their own rhythms, come together round the television screen.

There is a pseudo-liturgical rhythm to television time which marks it off from the patterns of daily living. At fixed points viewers keep tryst with their television sets — especially at TV news times. Viewers stay in touch with the nation and the outside world by tuning in to the news, which is a public symbol through which one version of reality is shared.

Because television is an electronic story-teller whose fishy eye is always on the look-out for spectacle, events when televised assume a high symbolic significance. The wedding of Prince Charles and Princess Diana, watched by an estimated eleven hundred million viewers throughout the world, came across as the traditional fable of the Prince and the Maiden. Winston Churchill's televised funeral had Wagnerian overtones as the old warrior sped on his way to Valhalla, loaded with honours. And millions of Americans wept openly as they watched the funeral of John F. Kennedy, the resplendent hero struck down at the height of his powers by a malign fate.

It is not just to great events that television gives symbolic significance. Any event framed by the small screen and happening in special space and time has a ritual aspect. And this ritual, by allowing the mass sharing of stories and events at a uniform time, is a major force for social integration. The flow of electronic signals affects the way people think collectively, not only about serious matters but also about the froth of life such as fashion, gossip and play.

Thus, if the religious muscles of secular man and woman are not exercised by traditional religion, they will be brought to bear on this other world of humanly created meaning, television, for we cannot survive without drama, pageant, play and fantasy. When formal religion is privatized and becomes preoccupied with esoteric imagery and ritual that is inaccessible to the generality of society, a popular piety springs up, searching for other ways of expressing faith. The starved imagination, like the empty belly, is remarkably catholic in its tastes. Writes Gregor Goethals, "Until institutional religion can excite the serious play of the soul and evoke the fullness of human passion, television will nurture our illusions of heroism and transcendence."[16]

It was the theologian Paul Tillich who first gave wide currency to the phrase "theology of culture" – he defined it as "the attempt to show the religious dimension in many special spheres of man's cultural activity". And Tillich was not using the word culture in any snobbish sense, to do simply with the fine arts or classics. In his understanding of the word, no one can be uncultured – cartoons both by da Vinci and Walt Disney, music both by Bach and Scott Joplin, literary epics both by Tolstoy and Wilbur Smith – all help to provide the symbols which feed the soul.

So however exasperated believers may get with television, they would be foolish to damn it as utterly demonic, as some moralists are wont to do. For even at its most crass it is still exercising human spiritual faculties which might otherwise wither away. Even a diet of pap keeps the digestive system working, so that when given the opportunity it can go to work on real red meat.

Double-Vision
For the first time in twenty years, I recently went to Lords to watch a test match. And I was bitterly disappointed – not by the quality of the play but by my restricted view of what was happening – by which I do not mean that I had a poor seat. But after watching cricket on television, I had become accustomed to a synoptic view of the action. Every time a wicket fell or the umpire made a controversial decision, I expected an action-replay in slow motion *and* the same shot from three different angles *and* an expert commentator to talk me through the sequence. In other words, the real world wasn't good enough. Things only happen once there, often in a flash, whereas by courtesy

of television's re-play capacity, I could analyse reality at leisure until its significance was clear to me.

Afficionados of cricket will contest hotly that opinion. The atmosphere of the real event is the thing, they insist, and there is no way television can communicate *that*. Maybe, but the truth is that television is no longer just a communications system or an entertainment medium. It creates its own cosmos, virtually an alternative form of reality.

Karl Marx said that all historical events happen twice; once as tragedy and again as comedy. Similarly, a new duality has entered the contemporary world. Things now happen twice – once *out there* and once *in here* on the television screen.

Those who think that the notion of television as an alternative cosmos is ludicrously over-stated might ponder the statistic which says that in the United States a significant number of people, especially the house-bound and the young, spend more hours watching television than doing any other single thing, not excluding sleeping. For the old, afraid to leave their homes in dangerous times, the machine in the corner has become their primary link with reality.

Whether or not television is as authentic an experience as what it records, it is increasingly becoming the authenticating experience. The American historian David Boorstin writes, "The television experience is what makes an issue live, what makes a politician into a statesman, what makes and unmakes a President, what makes an event catastrophic, what makes a question controversial and what makes a neighbourhood event significant."

During the Vietnam war, U.S. bomber pilots attacking Hanoi for the first time commonly described the anti-aircraft barrages and the fires on the ground as being "just like a World War Two movie!" – life and death reality was being judged by its approximation to film fantasy. We now live in an *Alice in Wonderland* where we switch with bewildering frequency between reality and illusion. "Tweedledee said to Alice, 'You won't make yourself a bit realer by crying . . . ' Alice replied, 'If I wasn't real, I wouldn't be able to cry!' 'I hope you don't think those are real tears?' interrupted Tweedledum crossly."

David Boorstin has adopted a term from ophthalmics to describe our need to keep an eye on two versions of reality. Our society, he says, is suffering from *diplopia*, which is a vision disorder that causes objects to appear twice. So the challenge to those concerned to improve the quality of life is to make things better, not in one but in two worlds or two parallel versions of reality – on and off the tube, for it is interaction between the two which determines the nature of reality.

All of this poses some interesting questions about Christian mission. However daunting the task may be, we know what is involved by way of worship, belief and witness in trying to claim the world for Christ. But what about that alternative cosmos, within whose warm, bright frontiers people spend a significant proportion of their waking hours? As Harvey Cox says, "Mass media culture is a religion, and we rarely get out of its temple." How is that world to be redeemed, or does such a notion take us into the surrealist realms of science fiction?

Only when the Church's thinking moves beyond the stage of regarding television as a more complicated form of the pulpit public address system – with endless fret about how believers sound and look and perform – will it be ready to face up to the true dimensions of the challenge. For Christianity is about God coming amongst us and establishing divine life in our neighbourhood, so that we discover what it is by struggling with it. A significant part of our neighbourhood in the contemporary world is television's electronic environment which wraps us round like a blanket. So that's where some of this struggling will have to be done in order to seize the Kingdom.

The rule must still be that full personal encounter is the norm of Christian mission. But what about those for whom the only meaningful encounter they make from one week's end to another is in rendezvous with their favourite television programmes and stars? Marshall McLuhan rhapsodized about the global village created by television, but it is the fake togetherness of a honeycomb of hermits' cells in a cave wall.

Just as television has blurred any unified perception of reality, so it has rendered virtually meaningless the distinction between public and private spheres of life. These tele-hermits will form one huge television audience, a secular ecclesia of awesome dimensions, congregated for a public event – yet they will be watching it in private, in isolated ones, twos and threes.

This mind-boggling state of affairs certainly suggests a sharp reversal of the order of priorities on the agendas of Christian mission – where "media" matters now occupy that sub-section of Any Other Business once devoted to pamphlets, visual aids and the up-dating of parish magazines.

ELEVEN

JESUS – THE PERFECT COMMUNICATOR?

I recently came across these sentences from the evangelical scholar and writer Oswald Sanders: "In their pages, the Evangelists present a portrait of a man, a real man who displays absolute perfection at every stage of development in every circumstance and relationship of life." Well, it seems to me that it would take some quite heroic feats of verbal gymnastics and textual surgery to explain gospel incidents which reveal Jesus to have displayed anything but "absolute perfection" – where he is all too human: harsh, impatient and sarcastic. But call that a difference in perspective.

Then Sanders goes on to rhapsodize about Jesus' preaching style – he is the perfect communicator, clear, vivid and simple, his artistry supremely demonstrated in the style and structure of the Sermon on the Mount: a plain guide to daily living – the model on which any young preacher should base his pulpit utterance. I venture to suggest that any preachers who modelled their pulpit style on Jesus would be rewarded with dwindling congregations, and not simply because they copied their Lord's harsh condemnations of the rich and conventionally pious, or made impossible spiritual demands on their people.

Leaving aside the carping point that what we know of Jesus' preaching from the gospels is a literary reconstruction of what the apostles remembered of his oratory, in no conventional sense of the term was Jesus a preacher at all. Utter clarity? Every theological library has shelves groaning with volumes whose generic theme might be paraphrased as "What did Jesus mean by . . . ?" Take just one example: his reference to the sin for which there shall be no forgiveness. What was it? To spend half an hour with the Bible commentators is to stagger away with a thick head. The only thing they are agreed upon is that the meaning is opaque and might refer to . . . or on the other hand . : . yet again. . . .

So what kind of preaching is this? With utter candour, the gospels report that Jesus' hearers often went away shaking their heads and trying to work out just what he was on about. His family certainly found him hard to understand; they were all set to have him put away in an asylum; and John the Baptist in prison couldn't decide from what he'd heard whether or not Jesus *was* the Messiah. No matter how often Jesus warned the disciples of his impending death, they were still astounded when it happened. That was certainly one message he didn't get across. The crowds who heard him gladly when he was doling out food and healing became a dwindling congregation when he offered only strong words.

Any elegant rhetorical structure we find in these gospel utterances is likely to be a polish applied by apostolic memory to the constant repetition of Jesus' original words. His sayings seem to have had all the character of extempore, even naïve speech; uncalculated, throbbing with dramatic immediacy and spoken both without regard for the consequences and with no thought for posterity. And he makes no concessions to the frailties of human understanding; no neat homiletical structure leads his hearers on from the plains to the mountain-top of truth.

Of course not. If we take seriously the Anglican theologian Austin Farrer's saying that Jesus did not think human thoughts divinely but divine thoughts humanly, what ought we to expect from Jesus but a radical otherness in speech and behaviour, which mocks that laudable desire on the part of preachers to think and utter human thoughts divinely? — for that is the very best the greatest human preacher can do.

Jesus could not be the model for any apprentice preacher; the scale, style and content of his speech is strictly inimitable. If he truly was, as the title of one of Bishop John Robinson's books puts it, "The Human Face of God", we would expect Jesus to look at the world through very different eyes from natural men or woman; to make judgements according to alien rules and to speak in riddles. For if as God says, "My thoughts are not your thoughts" then his way of incarnating those thoughts in words ought at least to sound very odd to our ears.

There is actually profound theology in the old saying that truth is stranger than fiction. Of couse it is, because fiction is always the product of a human mind which will work overtime to make a story congenial and understandable to other minds. But truth is a different matter. Because its source is outside ourselves, we must either accept it in whatever form it presents itself to us or turn it into fiction to make it more believable.

For the very best of motives, preachers are always prone to turn shocking truth into acceptable fiction. Whenever we come across an enigmatic saying in the gospel, in order to make it credible, we bend it a little, trim it at the edges, paraphrase it judiciously or even claim access to Jesus' mind and insist he was talking metaphorically. Our motives are entirely honourable but the effect is to rob his words of the trauma of the transcendent. We turn Jesus into the greatest preacher or teacher there has ever been, and in our naïvety imagine we are paying him some kind of compliment.

A visitor to an art gallery confronted by a painting whose title "Sunset over Battersea" is the only recognizable thing about it, can do a number of things. He can turn it upside down or sideways to check it was hung correctly in the first place. He can take a bus at dusk to Battersea, find the exact spot from which the artist painted the work and try to match his own perception with the painter's. What he cannot do is to change the painting's title to "Portrait of My Mother-in-Law" or "Scrambled Eggs".

The artist may be a genius or a colour-blind dauber in a high fever, but it is his way of looking at something and recording it that is sovereign. By all means advise him to see a doctor or take up another hobby, but there is no point in trying to convince him he was really painting something different from what he claims. And the artist is entitled to retort that you have an uneducated eye or an insensitive spirit, or that you have never seen Battersea from the perspective of his studio.

We preachers behave in a similar fashion when we collide with the more puzzling sayings or inexplicable actions of Jesus in the gospels. We try a little careful rearrangement of the narrative, or suggest alternative translations of the original Aramaic, or quote some giant of New Testament scholarship before whose awesome learning a simple Galilean carpenter would obviously bow and rephrase his gauche comments.

We are not allowed such options. It is the artist's conception of Battersea, or in this case, Jesus' understanding of the Kingdom of Heaven, that is sovereign. And we must either adjust our perspective to see things through his eyes or else have done with the whole business, but we cannot trim down his vision to our expectations. We are called to be heralds but not propagandists. We cannot rework the truth, only seek to interpret it.

Because Jesus thought divine thoughts humanly rather than human thoughts divinely, we *ought* to find the Gospel shocking in some parts, paradoxical in others, but always capable of deeper meanings than our casual scrutiny has elicited. Otherwise, Jesus was just the greatest preacher we ever heard multiplied by X.

Great biblical scholars who are so familiar with the text of the gospels that they could recite them word for word, have been known to confess that after a life-time's study, some truths continue to elude them whilst others break in on them unexpectedly. Long-familiar words, pondered a thousand times, inexplicably become charged with new meaning when studied yet again or heard in a different setting or matched against a contemporary situation which seems to be a commentary on them.

It is hard to resist the conclusion that the basic purpose of Jesus' preaching was not to enlighten or to inform but to shock – to shake his hearers awake, to rock them out of the comfortable tramlines of their usual existence and get them facing another way. So he does absolutely nothing to render his words more palatable. He makes no attempt to smooth over the disjunction between things divine and things human, or to lead people by gentle steps into the presence of a holy and transcendent God.

Jesus had no message in the usual sense of that term.

Jesus – The Perfect Communicator?

The radical theologian Don Cupitt wrote, "Jesus is hardly at all concerned with giving information or making predictions. On the contrary, his speech is religious action: he warns, summons, reveals, commands, promises and attacks, always with the intention of bringing about religious change in the hearer . . . it is the call to abandon *everything* and receive the reign of God."[17]

One of the great theologians of this century, P. T. Forsyth, once characterized preaching in an ordination address in 1909 as "acting on people". "It is not the Fatherhood of God you have to preach, but God the Father. You have not to preach about God to people, you must preach God *into* people. So true preaching is not telling people, but acting on people, making people." And it can't be done. Not by any formula or combination of words and ideas of human devising. This is the folly of preaching.

Christ himself was only able to preach God into a handful of people – until Calvary. There he preached the final, complete and unequivocal sermon – in silence. Unlike his more enigmatic sayings, this word could not be misunderstood. It could be ignored, rejected, but not misunderstood. It was perfect communication at infinite cost.

So the young preacher who looks to Christ as a model had better count the cost. The distinguishing feature of the Christian preacher who seeks to imitate the Nazarene orator is not silver-tongued eloquence but the marks he bears in his body of the dying of the Lord Jesus.

NOTES

1. Quoted by Neil Postman, *Amusing Ourselves to Death*, Heinemann, 1986, p. 118.
2. I am indebted to Alan Richardson's *Christian Apologetics*, SCM, 1950, chapter 8, for some of the ideas in this section.
3. In *The New Creation as Metropolis*, Macmillan, 1963.
4. Gerhard Leibholz, quoted in *The Shame and the Sacrifice*, Edwin Robertson, Hodder & Stoughton, 1987.
5. I owe this notion of TV as an electronic minstrel to Fiske and Hartley, *Reading Television*, Methuen, 1978, p. 85 et seq.
6. Rupert Davies, *Methodism*, Epworth, 1963, p. 95.
7. G. B. Caird, *The Language and Imagery of the Bible*, Duckworth, 1980, p. 176.
8. I drew some of my illustrations from Derek Elley's *The Epic Film*, Routledge & Kegan Paul, 1984.
9. Stephen May drew my attention to this image.
10. Harvey Cox, *The Feast of Fools*, Harvard, 1969, p. 142.
11. I think Malcolm Muggeridge coined the term.
12. I rely heavily on Sissela Bok's *Secrets*, Oxford, 1982, for both arguments and illustrations in this section.
13. Neil Postman, *Amusing Ourselves to Death*, Heinemann, 1986, p. 118.
14. *The Vocabulary of the Bible*, Lutterworth, 1958.
15. *Oh! What a Blow That Phantom Gave Me!*, Paladin, 1976, p. 12.
16. Gregor Goethals, *The TV Ritual*, Beacon, Boston, p. 84, to which I owe some of the themes in this section.
17. Don Cupitt, *Jesus and The Gospel of God*, Lutterworth, 1979, p. 68.

Wrestling with an Angel

COLIN MORRIS

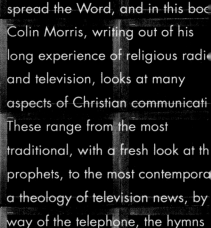

The mass media are used in various ways by Christians wanti to carry out Christ's command to spread the Word, and in this boc Colin Morris, writing out of his long experience of religious radi and television, looks at many aspects of Christian communicati These range from the most traditional, with a fresh look at th prophets, to the most contempora a theology of television news, by way of the telephone, the hymns Charles Wesley, the issue of viole on our TV screens, and a humoro look at the special temptations tho assail religious broadcasters.

A Fount Origina

Cover illustration by Leigh Hurlock

U.K .£4.99
AUS $13.95
N.Z. $20.95
(inc. GST)*
CAN $9.95
*rec price

ISBN 0-00-627507-9

00499

9 780006 275077